DIALOGUE WITH GOD

HEARING

BELIEVING

ENGAGING

RENDA BRUMBELOE

hearing   believing   engaging

Dialogue with God

Copyright © 2018 by Renda Brumbeloe All rights reserved.
No part of this publication may be reproduced, stored in a
retrieval system or transmitted in any way by any means, electronic, mechanical, photocopy, recording or otherwise without the prior permission of the author except as provided by USA copyright law.

Scripture quotations marked (niv) are taken from the *Holy Bible, New International Version®*. niv®. Copyright© 1973, 1978, 1984 by International Bible Society. Used by permission of Zondervan. All rights reserved.
Scripture quotations marked (nkjv) are taken from the *New King James Version®*. Copyright © 1982 by Thomas Nelson, Inc. Used by permission. All rights reserved.

Scripture quotations marked (kjv) are taken from the *Holy Bible, King James Version*, Cambridge, 1769. Used by permission. All rights reserved.
Scripture quotations marked (nasb) are taken from the *New American Standard Bible®*, Copyright © 1960, 1962, 1963, 1968, 1971, 1972, 1973, 1975, 1977, 1995 by The Lockman Foundation. Used by permission.

Scripture quotations marked (nlt) are taken from the *Holy Bible, New Living Translation,* copyright © 1996. Used by permission of Tyndale House Publishers, Inc., Wheaton, Illinois 60189. All rights reserved.
Scripture quotations marked (tniv) are taken from the *Holy Bible, Today's New International Version ®*. tniv®. Copyright© 2001, 2005 by International Bible Society. Used by permission of Zondervan. All rights reserved.

Scripture quotations marked (msg) are taken from *The Message.* Copyright © 1993, 1994, 1995, 1996, 2000, 2001, 2002. Used by permission of NavPress Publishing Group.
Scripture quotations marked (ncv) are taken from the *New Century Version®*. Copyright © 2005 by Thomas Nelson, Inc. Used by permission. All rights reserved.

Scripture quotations marked (hcsb) are taken from the *Holman Christian Standard Bible®*, Copyright © 1999, 2000, 2002, 2003 by Holman Bible Publishers. Used by permission. Holman Christian Standard Bible®, Holman CSB®, and HCSB® are federally registered trademarks of Holman Bible Publishers.

Published by CreateSpace.com; Amazon.com
Published by Renda Brumbeloe; 3DSOUNDSTUDIOS, 2018. All rights reserved.
Cover design by Scott Soliz; Published in the United States of America
ISBN-13: 978-0692103651 (Custom Universal) ISBN069103651
1. Religion, Christian Life, Devotional
2. Religion, Christian Life, Spiritual Growth
04.25.18

hearing   believing   engaging

DIALOGUE WITH GOD

Recommendations

Knowing the writer of this book enhances its message even more. Here is a book that will inspire you to a deeper relationship with God through conversation with God and purposeful living for God. The illustrations and applications are outstanding. This writing is rather similar to the analogy of C. S. Lewis, who has had a large influence in shapingthe author's rationale. Sit back, read and reread, and then deeply reflect upon God and his purpose for our lives.

Lyle G. Parker: Missionary, Retired Elder, Office Manager-Abogados Parker & Parker, P.A., Kansas City, KS

Over the years I have listened for the voice of God. He has spoken to me through his word, fellow believers and open doors, but most often there has been a "gentle whisper" like the prophet Elijah heard. In *Dialogue with God*, Renda Brumbeloe reminds us that we were made for dialogue and who better to dialogue with than our loving Father. He then challenges us to move beyond dialogue to a life of submission to that small, still voice of an infinite God. In these written words you might find a new way of life.

Rick Harvey Senior PastorBethany First Church

In his book, "Dialogue with God", Renda Brumbeloe shares the connection of faith in our Lord with the need for faith to show itself by its behaviors. The action of faith and works is never at odds with each other. Faith is not just the beginning of the Christian life but also its continuation.

H. Lamar Smith Pastor
    Author; http://christourholyway.com

"This is a book for persons who seriously want to know God and foster a relationship with the Divine. The author uses his experiences as professional musician, airline pilot, and avid reader to demonstrate what a balanced Christian life looks like. For anyone who would desire a closer relationship with God, this personal account of one person's search for such provides an example of the dedication required to achieve such a worthy goal. Highly recommend!"

Loren Gresham, PhD,
President Emeritus of Southern Nazarene University

ACKNOWLEDGEMENTS

I acknowledge that writing a *Dialogue with God*, is formidable and heavy when you begin the reality and honesty of writing your thoughts on paper.

One of my agnostic "philosophical friends"asked me the title of my book. Then he abruptly asked me, "Well, what is He saying to you?"

"The same things He says to you and all of us." God's unexpected words of mercy, grace and judgment are written in the rocks, hills and hearts and history books. However writing this dialogue is making me listen more intently than ever. That is the hard part."

It has now been several months since that encounter with my friend and I have been reassured after putting the manuscript away and coming back to words that did not seem to be mine. And I knew I had to keep writing. The words were cogent and faithful to my dialogue with God. I now know that my dialogue is not just thought, but is alive in my faith of daily living.

With friends and family who invest their talents and time in reading manuscripts and encouraging excellence and clarity, I give love and gratitude. Friends who, for fifteen years, have read and responded to my weekly Morning Musing blog and have responded often are too numerous to list.

Close friends like Lyle and Joann Parker, who have shown early valued guidance in reading this manuscript, and my long-time mentor and encourager, Dr. Thomas Barnard, for his grammatical edits and pertinent questions and for writing the Preface of this book, mere thanks is not adequate. And for Ashley Luckett, master editor of my book, *Life at 35,000 Feet,* and this new book, *Dialogue with God*, I am grateful for demanding my best presentation and communication. And to my multi-talented grand-daughter, Isabella Ferguson, for final layout and important edit corrections and clarity, I cannot thank enough. Finally, to Sharon, my resourceful wife, who quietly provokes the clarity of words and meaning, I am most grateful.

PREFACE

I am pleased to recommend Renda Brumbeloe's newest book, *Dialogue with God*. Like in his previous book, *Life At 35,000 Feet*, *Dialogue* contains stories about commercial flying that alone are worth the price of the book. Everything else in these pages is theologically sound and biblically based, and Renda approaches his subject with the commitment to excellence that has characterized his entire adult life.

Before turning to commercial flying, Renda had established his reputation as an exceptional church musician and concert pianist. But he loved to fly and flying commercially became his dream and professional priority. When most dads were working primarily to provide things for their kids, Renda did that as well as pursuing a new vocation at 35,000 feet. In 2002, Renda retired from United Airlines following a distinguished career as Captain on the Boeing 727.

Following retirement, Renda wanted to write a few stories for his family about his flying experiences. He would continue to write eclectically —first, in weekly musings he sent to a growing list of readers, and subsequently in essays and books. Since youth, Renda accumulated and read the writings of famous theologians and philosophers from around the world. You will find some of their writings throughout *Dialogue*.

In *Dialogue*, Renda has taken on serious subjects to explore. While admitting his lack of theological training and credentials, Renda was unafraid to tackle many of the hot topics that are drawing attention in seminars, religious gatherings, and social media today. You may not agree with all of his conclusions, but you will admire him for his fervor.

Prepare yourself for a flight into God's World.

Thomas Elliott Barnard – M.A., Ed D

hearing   believing   engaging

TABLE OF CONTENTS

RECOMMENDATIONS   4

ACKNOWLEDGMENTS   5

PREFACE   6

TABLE OF CONTENTS   7

FOREWORD   10

LOOKING IN THE REAR-VIEW MIRROR   12

PURPOSE   15

CAPTAINS PEROGATIVE   21

DIALOGUE OF REALITY   27

LANDING AT THE WRONG CONCLUSION   34

GOD SPEAKS TRUTH THROUGH HIS WORD   39

THE GOD OF THE FIRST AND LAST   40

THE ETERNAL METEOROLOGIST   42

THE YES-OR-NO QUESTION   44

A WONDERFUL DIALOGUE IS BORN   46

GET IT RIGHT   49

THE STORY OF JOB   51

ENCROACHING DARKNESS AND LOSS OF VISIBILITY   53

THE MAGNETIC COMPASS   54

THE NATURAL AND SPIRITUAL LAWS OF GOD   56

THE REVEALED DIALOGUE   59

MORALITY AND POLITICAL CORRECTNESS   60

MORALITY AND THE LAWS OF PHYSICS   61

TRUTH AND VALUE SYSTEMS   62

hearing   believing   engaging

PART TWO   67
FAITH   67
SIGNS OF THE TIMES   69
THE SILENCE IS DEAFENING   73
QUESTIONS THAT NEED ANSWERS   74
FROM DARKNESS TO LIGHT   78
A BEGUILED CULTURE   80
THE BEGUILING LIGHT   83
FAITH IS A HARD WORD   87
THE MOMENT OF TRUTH   88
IMPORTANT MESSAGES OF FAITH   89
THE MESSAGE OF THE CENTER LINE   89
THE MESSAGE OF CONTAMINATED FUEL   91
TOOLS FOR CHRISTIAN LIVING   93
YES, NO OR MAYBE   95
FAITH AND RELEVANCE   96
WHAT IS FAITH   98
REPENTANCE   99
UNCERTAINTY AND FAITH   102
THE LINE IN THE SANDS OF TIME   103
THE PIECES OF FAITH   105
CONTINUING FAITH   106

hearing   believing   engaging

A PERSONAL DIALOGUE   108

KNOWING AND TRUSTING   110

WHAT FAITH   114

STRETCHING OUR FAITH MUSCLES   116

AN EXERCISE OF THANKSGIVING AND PRAISE   117

CONFESSION LOVE OBEDIENCE   119

FAITH THAT DISPELS OUR FEARS   121

THE UNITY OF FAITH, FELLOWSHIP AND WORSHIP   122

FINDING REST   124

GO OR NO GO   125

EPILOGUE   128

THE VISIBLE AND INVISIBLE CHURCH   129

ONE FINAL AIRLINE STORY   132

A DAY WITH GOD   134

GROUP DISCUSSION STUDY GUIDE   136

A FAITH-BUILDING DIALOGUE FROM THE RESURRECTION   140

QUOTABLES   141

hearing   believing   engaging

FOREWORD

Some people prefer the aisle seats on airplanes. When given an option, I always choose the window. My travels have kept me on airplanes often in the last 40 years and my fellow passengers have provided me with a host of stories, actually quite a few of which have found their way into a sermon. Stories about divine appointments when I was convinced God gave me an opportunity to make a friend and talk about what it means to have a personal relationship with Jesus. I have watched people in tears when we were in long periods of turbulence over the North Atlantic and people share their stories of success and failure at 37,000 feet. I love stories and my friend, Renda Brumbeloe, packs his wonderful book, *Dialogue with God*, full of stories that beautifully illustrate the most important story ever told, our relationship with God.

Though never a pilot or even an airline employee, I am completely comfortable in the sky. I remain amazed that the kind of monstrous passenger planes captained by Renda can break the plane of gravity and soar across the heavens and even though I don't understand all the physics involved, I love the privilege and possibilities provided by the airline industry. Airlines have allowed me to see a great deal of God's earthly creation and time in the sky provides some wonderful opportunities to dialogue with God.

Recently as I settled into my window seat for a short flight from Houston Intercontinental to Dallas-Fort Worth, I decided to close my eyes and catch a quick nap. Unfortunately, the gentleman seated next to me on the aisle was preventing me from getting comfortable. The more I attempted to relax, the more he squirmed in his seat. While I didn't want to stare at him, he was making me very nervous as he checked his watch, looked out the plane window, and continued to be restless. Finally, he apologized and blurted out, "I hate to fly!" Now his nervousness made sense. I asked him how often he had to fly. His response surprised me, "every week."

Turns out he was a salesman and his territory required him to board multiple planes each week. His transparency about this fear led to a great conversation with a most memorable line from my new friend, "If I knew the pilot, I would not be nearly as afraid."

His statement is true about life too! Renda, knows our pilot, Jesus Christ, personally. He has studied the greatest selling book of all time, God's Holy Word, and Renda knows that we can know and trust the One who knows us and loves us. *Dialogue with God* will keep you fully engaged as you consider your story and how God continues to intersect and at times interrupt your life. You will learn from Renda's experience and be challenged to love God with all your heart.

Leonardo da Vinci wrote, "Once you have tasted flight, you will forever walk the earth with your eyes turned skyward, for there you have been, and there you will always long to return." Spend time in this book and you will learn how much Renda loves flying. You will also learn how much he loves Jesus. I believe that is why he writes. He wants us to love Jesus too!

Dr. Keith Newman, President,
Southern Nazarene University

hearing   believing   engaging

LOOKING IN THE REAR-VIEW MIRROR

... THIS IS THE NARRATIVE, much I will not tell, but it was my heart's desire... I wanted to fly for the airlines, the big iron.

Airplanes captured my eyes and imagination, but music and piano were in my ears and in my heart.

My teacher said I had perfect pitch... However, as a teenager, I realized I had two dreams – piano and airline flying. What about college plans? Should I commit to the Air Force during college or would I wash out? Was it too far a stretch to consider the Air Force as an eventual pathway to the airlines?

... I was conflicted. My heart burned within me ... Psalm 39:3

Beethoven's Opus 57 Piano Sonata, (The Appassionato) helped to made my decision when I first heard it one night on the radio.

So, I entered college at age eighteen to major in theory and piano performance. It was a challenging decision. It demanded all my time. After graduation, I accepted a teaching position while continuing my Master's Degree. I enjoyed great satisfaction and synergy in piano and in training choirs and working with talented musicians. However, the aviation dream was not dead, but still lying in wait.

After college, I added to my private license and passed commercial and flight instructor ratings. Please understand, this is far from the experience and flight time required of an airline transport pilot (ATP).

The aviation dream would not die. It would be a long journey and would require stepping stones. I studied hard and hoped to get my chance, understanding how competitive the airline job offers could be and knew that even if qualified, I might never get an airline interview.

So, life goes on and we use the gifts that God gives us. Meanwhile, we walk through the doors of opportunities that come, and God is there.

As a young basic flight instructor, I said to my students, "Do you really want to learn to fly? Then you must burn the midnight oil. Study! Be willing to turn the pages. Love it and keep the dream alive." I was saying this to myself as well.

An airline career seemed an impossible path requiring years of big corporate jet flying or heavy military experience of which I had none.

I eventually achieved the coveted airline transport rating, plenty of flight experience, and flight instructing corporate job to complement my college degrees but it still seemed barely enough to get any airline attention—no heavy iron. I began crossing every "t "and dotting every "I" with applications. Then I had an unexpected curve in the road:

A major airline offered me a training slot!

That meant after initial training I could be on reserve duty for who knew how long. Maybe years. Now with two small daughters in elementary school, it blindsided me. I could not bear the thought of being a part-time father away from home the best part of every week and missing the joy of seeing my young daughters grow up, pushing their swings, hearing their laughter, and playing their games.
A voice in my head said, "Do not mess up what you can never catch up. Besides, there is presently heavy turbulence in the airline industry." Yes, I was in conflict again.

I knew that voice was an unwanted but a timely dialogue, so at the last minute I picked up the phone and said, "I cannot make the training date in two weeks. Please call me for the next class date." I hung up and cried for most of thirty-six hours. You only get one shot for an opportunity like this. I had just put scissors to my dream that still would not die.

All the hard work and study was going up in smoke. I had qualified myself and hesitated. What had I done? In hindsight, God had intervened in my plans and dreams. After all, I could not foresee or prophesy what God had planned for me.

I was experiencing a wonderful decade of fulfillment in my life that I had not seen coming. It was reality and I almost missed it.

Meanwhile, I would continue my music ministry career and business aviation. Little did I know that God's future timing would be much better. I would get a second chance, and God's timing.

Why am I telling this brief narrative? Looking back, it is the serious business of "scripting our lives," knowing what we believe and to what we commit.

I can see clearly now, this was the beginning of a *Dialogue with God* and one I now write. It was seeing reality and God's purpose for my life in faith for the future.

Whatever you do in life,

you will believe something important.

When a Captain walks onto his airplane, his passengers put their faith in him. What does he believe then? What would I believe if I were the captain?

When my airplane begins to bounce around and my world gets turbulent, it could be my hand. Be ready for it.

Meanwhile, follow the reality of God in your life. Sometimes we see the future by looking in the rear-view mirror, as God has different ways to call us to reality.

I am now a retired airline Captain with 21,000 hours in the air. The biographical sketches in this book intend to explain how I have grown to appreciate my upbringing and youth as I discovered a multi-layered vocation.

My mother loved her children with a divine love from God. She lived only for the joy of her family, our happiness and well-being. She gave herself completely to raising seven children and believing God's mercies.

At age 28, my father accepted the call of God in his life after a God-ordained encounter with a minister. He followed in his grandfather's footsteps, and with conviction, he entered the ministry that changed the course of our family's future. My parents' constant dialogue to me as a teenager was, "Go for it. Follow your dreams, but do not forget God."

What better way to experience the attributes of God? Seeing your dreams come true as a new-hire airline pilot and looking at the vast world through the windshield of the planes you always wanted to fly.

The rear-view mirror is a true view of where we have been. It is a moral view, revealing our moral clarity. All our hard decisions have become a reality that we now face. Yes, we are flawed and conflicted.

The rear-view mirror is an opportunity to reduce our conflict and adjust our world view to the Master Captain of our future.

PART 1
PURPOSE

God does not come to us in a box. We cannot unpack God, nor can we construct Him. He comes to us in dialogue and surprises. We have to face reality.

We are made to dialogue. It is human nature. We talk to each other and ourselves as well. Sometimes we just mutter. We can monologue about injustices and wrong decisions we make. Seldom does anyone want to hear our negative self.

What is a dialogue anyway? Certainly not complaining. It is an exchange of information. It brings understanding and relationship to both who are listening.

If you really want to be heard, let your thoughts become a dialogue with someone like a good friend who will give you a good hearing and not judge you. You learn more in a dialogue than talking to yourself.

What is better than conversation with a friend anyway, someone who matters? Like God! He already knows us, so He listens well. He leads us into truth that we could never discover on our own. As you read, you will soon find that I raise many questions about the nature of God. I also ask questions about faith. However, I ask the overall question of what we believe about a

Creator God who created us in His image. Wow, that opens to us many great possibilities.

I am writing to people of faith and also to skeptics and young people who have discarded the faith of their youth. And to all of us, I ask this question: Besides basic needs of life, what is the most important thing that drives you as you rise or begin your day?

As you read this book I hope that your questions and answers might become important and clear to you.

Can we have a dialogue with an invisible God? Why not? He created us. He gave us His Word of Life. He gave us our life and His Holy Spirit. We did nothing for that gift. However, a dialogue means we must listen, intensely and sometimes painfully.

A WORD TO SKEPTICS: I have lived long enough to learn that it is easy to have flawed logic and blind spots in things you believe or wish for. I have experienced flawed belief in both the secular workplace and within the walls of a church fellowship.

A WORD TO BELIEVERS: We can sincerely believe anything and be deceived. But the fact is, truth will jump out and surprise us when we are least expecting it. That is the reason for the Holy Spirit, of whom Jesus said, "He will lead you into all truth" (John 16:13) God's truth is independent of belief systems and better than life experiences.

A WORD TO THOSE WHO HAVE DISCARDED THEIR FAITH: In this age of relativism, amid political correctness of our culture, some people have lost their clear message and many young people no longer know what they believe.

How does this happen? By taking steps down the ladder of belief. Discarding convictions, you once held sacred.

Losing your view of eternity. a step down the ladder of belief.

Yielding to a careless culture.

Salvation unimportant

hearing   believing   engaging

...And another step down. *Repentance, Morality, Sin, Honesty,* And the ladder of faith begins to lose its importance. We need the Holy Spirit's leading to know what is true.

Here are two important things to say at the outset.

First, I do not write as a trained theologian. However, God says He brings His Word to our remembrance.

God's Word has been presented to us in dialogue since the creation of man. There has never been a better time or more ways to read God's Word.

Language changes through every age. The result can build a shell around the original language and meaning. Still, the Scriptures stand alone in truth and we can mistake them.

The second thing is the very possibility of a dialogue with God. When someone tells me God told them something, my first reaction to the idea is to hold it at bay, to be skeptical. Then I remember how God has spoken to me. And for sure, I believe that God gives us secrets into our future.

How can we have a daily dialogue with God? We read over and over again that "God appeared" and "God said" and "God continued." That sounds like a dialogue about to break out, does it not?

God's Word is the password that opens our

dialogue box if we will just "boot up."

God is always nearby (like in the Garden of Eden with Adam and Eve) when we are not aware, making invisible appearances in our lives and even audibly in our ears. In that sense, we have all been there in the Garden, hearing His gentle urging.

Moreover, He gives us reasons for faith... even when we are distracted if we will see it. For example, to hear and participate in a dialogue like Adam and Eve did in the Garden of Eden, God's Paradise, that is until the serpent got in their way. What a real dialogue and drama recorded there. Yes, we have been there, and God's nearness sometimes says we have a lot to learn.

Our dialogue with God demands both reason and faith. The Holy Bible is a book that requires both reason and faith. It is both a reasonable book and a faithful book.

I invite you to engage in conversation and discuss life, truth, science, and faith with a loving God who claims us as His highest creation and to join in a dialogue that began long ago with the Word of God, in history and prophecy.

Part 1 of this book demonstrates our predicament, our "as is" state of being-original sin. We have freewill to be our own person and even decide for ourselves without regard to others.

It all began with Adam and Eve and the Great Deception when the serpent lied to them. Then great deception led to great doubt and denial. It always does. That is Satan's method. Something was wrong. God spoke up.

We are like Adam and Eve in the Garden. We have seen the fruit tree and responded modernly,

"It is what it is."

Putting aside the reality of the fruit tree, they ignored God's instruction. Yes, they missed it. However, the serpent spoke and forced them into a dialogue with God, our Creator.

We make good choices and certainly some bad decisions with our freedom to choose.

Like Adam and Eve, we consider the world our playground, our opportunities and our philosophy. Then we discover we have to answer to another authority, the fruit tree, and through the Tree of Knowledge, we are aware of God's righteousness and our fallen condition. Yes, we are flawed and conflicted.

The rear-view mirror is an opportunity to reduce our conflict and adjust our worldview back to the Master Creator of our future.

When we are born, we learn about good and evil, right and wrong, love and hate, morality and immorality. We learn to dialogue about life "as is", and as it unfolds. What is this un-asked-for mystery of life anyway?

Who is God? What are his attributes? Is He real? Why do we feel condemned? Why are we in conflict? Can we know the purpose of our life?

There are no "what ifs" with God.

We find ourselves in an involuntary dialogue because God speaks even when we are not listening. The dialogue has never stopped and points to the eternal "wireless connection" that God gives us if we will engage.

Part 2 of this book discusses faith and our discovery when the light of God begins to dawn on us. We gain wisdom when we look beyond ourselves and find our personal philosophy is not enough. Our culture is a poor teacher of reality. Culture makes honesty more difficult. However, faith unlocks the door to reality.

Philosophy of thought often is a forgery of the truth.

One voice in our conscience tells us truth. Another voice says we cannot handle the truth or even know the truth, that our past is only mythology and truth is religious symbolism, that faith and fact only beguile us and there are no absolutes.

However, that makes the dialogue about us and not about God. That is far off the mark of God's purpose for us.

God's truth is not enabled by our intellect. It is enabled through obedience to God's laws and His Holy Spirit Who leads us into truth.

In the same manner of how an aircraft flight manual gives truth to the checklist and design how an airplane flies, the Holy Scriptures is not subject to the reader's thinking, life experiences, biases or understanding of human life.

However, some contemporary readers often take the latitude that God's Word is open to whatever interpretation they glean from the narrative (no absolute truth). To such a reading, for them there is no hard truth, but whatever truth they read into the passage.

In fact, I find this reasoning of the Scriptures to be paltry and shallow to both man and God.

God's Word simply cannot mean whatever we conveniently interpret it to mean. "For who has known the mind of the Lord, or who has been his counselor" (Romans 11:34)? Is not "God's Word is forever settled in heaven." (Psalm 119:89)

The same is true for the design of space craft that operate at the edge of God's known and discoverable laws of physics.

Since 1957 when Russia launched Sputnik 1, and the first human in orbit in 1961, a specific a flight manual has been written for each of the hundreds of following space flight endeavors.

Here is the point, God created man in His own image and provides a specific physical and spiritual manual for all human life. The hairs of our head are numbered, and the allotment of days are known, and salvation is offered in our free will to say yes or no to God.

As a side note, consider this: If a professional juggler can demonstrate a microcosm of God's laws of physics in a masterful way (five balls in the air with two hands and catching them behind his back), why should I give any credence to someone who discounts God's Word being firm and true? I can believe that it really does reveal truth. Such thinking otherwise reveals that we live in a small universe and have not arrived at the table of reality.

hearing   believing   engaging

CAPTAINS PREROGATIVE

Let me tell you a personal flight story that is a bit difficult for me. This event happened when I was a first officer; however, as I have relived some of my flying memories, this flight still haunts me.

I was in the process of planning my transition to the Captain's seat and was forming a personal culture of flight safety, not to push the parameters of flight even though it fell within legal limitations. This would not be a formula but a mentality and would become my number-one Captain responsibility to my flight crew and the flying public. Making tough flight decisions has long been called "Captain's Prerogative." However, this is complicated by these four words: "*staying legal and staying alive.*" (Smile only momentarily, thank you.) I have experienced private confession is good for the soul.

Often, justifying our actions so that confession is not needed seems to be the easy way to go. In other words, if we can show we are being "reasonable and provide adequate grounds for the plan of action we are taking," we do not need confession for the action that we decide upon. Hmm. But is it?

Be reasonable and provide adequate grounds for the plan of action we are taking?

Those are the words that bothered me.

Reasonable and adequate grounds. What does that even mean? How is it interpreted? Let me just say it straight up: "We are not autonomous." We have no exemptions.

Here is the story:

We were flying into D.C. (Reagan National) and the landing winds were at max demonstrated crosswinds limit.

The Captain asked me if I was comfortable to execute the landing. I knew, as all airline pilots do, that a strong left crosswind landing, executed from the right seat (first officer seat), provides better visibility of the runway from the flight deck because of cockpit tilt and crab angles required to maintain the runway center line in those crosswind conditions.

I told him, "Yes, sir. No offense to you, but I'd rather do the landing than watch the landing." I think he was relieved. I know I was.

We told the passengers that we might have to divert to Baltimore because of high winds as we watched an American flight execute a go-around procedure, three miles in front of us.

Actually, Baltimore weather wasn't much better. Our winds were reported 270 degrees at 32 knots with gusts to 42. I suggested we request runway 33, the short runway, (330 degrees) which was only a sixty-degree crosswind. Woo Hoo!

I re-briefed the approach and landing and made it very clear that I had no expectation of touching down but just to shoot the approach to take a look. I knew at the last second, we might continue and touch down. (In reality this is flirting with the runway because that's what pilots do: WE LAND!) Pilots defend this thinking because all landings have the mentality of a go-around even in normal conditions.

All the way down the final approach we were buffeted by the swirling winds. Something was gnawing at the back of my brain, I felt like I was rewriting the flight manual, although we were still legal at this point.

Eighty feet above the runway, I added power and kicked right rudder to align the aircraft nose with the runway and announced, "I'm at right rudder limits." It was momentary, so I continued the approach. We were lined up on the runway center line at near maximum left bank. "50-30-10," sang out the radar altimeter; we touched down. It was hard work, but it was working out so far.

I released back pressure on the controls, deployed the ground spoilers, went into reverse thrust while applying full ailerons into the wind, and braked to a motivated stop while fighting to stay on the center line with the rudder pedals—it had to happen quick. We had executed a max-performance crosswind landing on runway 33 using only 3,500 feet rollout.

It seemed like an eternity but was only a few seconds. "You've got the airplane, Captain," I said as we approached the exit at end of the runway.

Then I realized I was breathing heavy. Flying doesn't have to be that much work. However, I had justified my action for the passengers, and maybe even stretched my previously demonstrated flying skills momentarily.

I could hear the "culture" cheering in the passenger cabin. They were glad we didn't divert. I felt some pride and satisfaction, but then I actually felt ashamed as I heard their response. Perhaps I had landed because of their expectations. Maybe we had bowed to cultural expectations. LAND! After all, I could have suggested to the Captain that we divert to another more suitable airport.

The haunting question remains: "Did we flirt with limitations that day?" We definitely dedicated our knowledge to a smaller framework while dealing with a bad crosswind.

When we arrived at the gate and set the parking brake, as I released my seatbelt, I decided this: "I've been there, I've done that, and I do not have to do it again ever!"

That would become my "Captain Prerogative," my personal culture of flight safety. As long as I fly, never push the limits. If a limitation is in the flight manual, it is there for a purpose.

I later told this story to a company Captain that I didn't know very well. He was not impressed! He said, "You did not have to do that!" Then he added, "As you gain experience, you will get more conservative, not more liberal. That's what keeps us all safe." And I thought to myself, *Yes, that is living in the spirit of the flight manual.*

"You did not have to do that" kept ringing in my head. In other words, what he meant was: safety is the ultimate motivation. Safety rises above all other motivations. Safety cannot be relegated to a smaller framework or a one-time disregard for pushing the safety envelope.

Although my Captain had trusted me to fly the approach into National Airport and we were able to land, I've been haunted reliving our decisions that day and their implications. I'm convinced that we made the wrong decision, flirting with crosswind limits and operating with the wrong motivation. I was too agreeable with the Captain and haven't flown that close to crosswind limits since then.

And so, I arrive at my reason for relating this story now.

It has become the genesis in my *Dialogue with God* and the supreme lesson I began to discover that day. This may be the most important thing I say in this manuscript.

Spiritual living is not by crosswind formula. God is not a formula. Captain Prerogative is not determined by formula.

I started the approach that afternoon into Washington D.C. believing in the absolute truth of God's physical laws of the universe. In other words, I am subject to God's Laws and God's Love at the same time.

The haunting question remains: "Did we disregard safety that day?"

"You did not have to do that" kept ringing in my head and it felt like I had yielded to temptation.

So, this is my synopsis and spiritual application.

Flying the approach to landing that afternoon was within legal parameters of the Flight Operating Manual. However, legality is not always the determinant. *(Suppose this might be true in other serious events of life?)*

Pilots deal with these decisions successfully every day, and most decisions are made before the event begins. *(Suppose this could be true in daily decisions?)*

Surely God's physical laws are for our protection and prove his love for us. If I break God's physical law, am I also disregarding His love?

Was it faith that made my decision to chalenge that strong crosswind that afternoon? I do not know. *(What drives most of our daily decisions?)*

When I arose that morning and put on my shoes, was I driven by faith? Did I know I would tamper with important crosswind limits?

Finally, how should we practice the Christian life in the framework of our challenging culture?

I recently read again Wilbur Wilberforce's book, *Real Christianity*. Although written more than 200 years ago, he develops the way we tend to practice the Christian life in the framework of our culture. And that is the point in our temptation of remaking Christianity to fit our present moment, instead of the living in the guidance of the Holy Spirit, the clarity of the Ten Commandments and in holiness before the Lord.

Wilberforce says, for the Christian, "the Holy Spirit is our ultimate motivation." In other words, like safety, the Holy Spirit rises above all other motivations. The Holy Spirit cannot be relegated to a smaller framework in our lives. I say again. We are not autonomous. The Holy Spirit is not a formula.

God is unmeasurable.

Likewise, a true believer does not live his or her life in both sacred and secular frameworks. As we gain growth in the Christian life, our standards will get tighter, not more liberal. We simply do not have to do some things. We love God more. There are some things that we will not entertain anymore

Here are Wilberforce's thoughts:

"We wrongly assume if I meet my religious obligations (as in a legal crosswind limitation) I am free to live my life as I wish. Thus, the reality and work of the Holy Spirit are held captive in a diminished role in our lives." Authentic faith is not allowed to expand and possess more of us. Wow!

When Christ our Lord is not free to possess more and more of who we are, the tendency over time is to take even what we have placed within the smaller framework and move it out into the larger context of our lives. We will actually regress in authentic spirituality...living like the culture lives and not knowing what we believe. The space occupied by active faith will diminish over time, until it is hardly active at all.

Holy and confessional living disappears and contrition is rarely expressed. And if we have not made that commitment, we may never make that decision.

Wilberforce is right. This is the genesis of cultural Christianity: waking up and realizing that we have slowly succumbed to making Christianity what we think what it ought to be, or worse, what we want it to be. The bottom line: "We do not know what we believe."

Wilberforce speaks to principles critical to living an authentic Christian life:

He passionately describes how the essential beliefs of authentic Christianity have been distorted (for example in my flight analogy, it's okay to try to land).

He clearly shows how concepts of sin, evil and depravity have been watered down (as in crosswind limitations can't be that important). Go ahead and take a look.

He challenges Christians to maintain a biblical lifestyle. (fly by the spirit of the Book) Again, we are not autonomous. Spiritual living goes beyond formula.

Dear Lord, dear merciful Lord, thank you for being with us. Protect us. Help us. Let us not bow to the cultural crosswinds that buffet our lives. Help us to live fully in the ultimate and infinite motivation of Your Holy Spirit. Let us hear Your continuing dialogue.

hearing　　believing　　engaging

A DIALOGUE OF REALITY

In all Life, we learn many things by faith

And then by fact

It is important to remember the things we learn by faith.

Reminiscing and asking questions is a great way to dialogue with a friend.

Skeptics will read these words. Hang with me. Let's talk this through. Here is a portion of my continued dialogue with Captain Bill.

"Bill, I know you have foregone church attendance and rejected the lifestyle of your youth, and your education continues to drive you. We've talked about that before and of course, that is important. However, do not throw away your family ties and memories of your youth. . . Never forget your roots, where you came from. Our past brings truth and meaning to our future. And know, that God does and will, reveal our future. That is the nature of his dialogue."

Here is an example. The Apostle Paul never forgot he was a Roman Jew and once a great unbeliever and persecutor of Christians. He wrote these words of great faith, after his experience on the road to Damascus.

"For, who can know the mind of God? Or who has been his counsellor?" (Romans 11:34; The Message, Eugene Peterson)

Here is another paraphrase of this scripture: *"Is there anyone around who can explain God? Anyone smart enough to tell him what to do? Anyone who has done him such a huge favor that God has to ask his advice?"*

The Past, Present and Future is God's

total definition of Time.

hearing   believing   engaging

Being a reflective person, as Daniel Taylor speaks about in his book *The Myth of Certainty*, I do not readily accept all that I hear spoken in educational, philosophical and religious circles.

However, I believe faith is an important...no, I believe faith is *the* most important part of our lives. Almost everything, including science and invention, is discovered by faith and proven by fact. In the same manner I have faith in the eternal miraculous God of reality.   I continued my conversation with Captain Bill.

"Bill, no doubt, you have learned many things in your life that you learned first by faith and then confirmed by fact. How exciting and confirming is reality."

When I was young, my gregarious friend David would say in conversation, "Are you for real?" Then he would chuckle. With that question, he would take the dialogue into his court and would laugh and joke and bring me to reality. He was highly entertaining, all of his six-foot-ten frame. He knew how faith became fact.

C.S. Lewis, one of the greatest literary minds of the twentieth century, commented that one should *"never ask of anything 'if it is real?' for everything is real. The proper question is "a real what?"* (C.S. Lewis, Letters to Malcolm, Chiefly on Prayer,1992; New York, Harcourt).

Lewis is more than suggesting here to skeptics that we cannot believe in honesty if we cannot believe in reality. What a great, but dreadful thought! Quoting C.S. Lewis again, from his autobiography, *Surprised by Joy:*

"Truth is discovered

when thought conforms to reality."

Yet we live in a world that is flush with relativism (relativism is a short-mutated reality) and a philosophy that says knowledge, truth and morality are debatable.

hearing   believing   engaging

This folly says, "What is true for you is not necessarily true for me. "Absolutes are not knowable." It is so easy to be proud of our liberated thinking. However,

How far have we fallen from the table of reality? This kind of "liberation thinking" has infiltrated our culture and modern churches. And then you find it sways your simple logic. Next up is honesty and reality! And then we are in trouble. All those who deny the fallen nature of the human race naively ignore reality. And the evidence today is overwhelming. Worse still, without reality, honesty is impossible.

G.K. Chesterton said, "The tragedy of a liar **is not** that he does not tell the truth, but that he cannot even know the truth."

The modern church and culture are rife with this belief system, full of man's ideas, unrealistic of even knowing God's Word, while they mis-interpret it.

The Gnostics had the same problem as discovered by the Apostle Paul in Athens. They were reading the Torah amid all the idols and debauchery in the city. It was liberation theology. It started with congratulating themselves for their success and attainment. Church became fun. Read Acts 17:15-34 and weep with Paul. Lord, let us not become like the church in Athens. It was the fake church.

We live in this present day when our rights and offenses seem to be on the tip of our tongue. As a by-product of political correctness, are we so self-absorbed?

However, the real Church is alive and well, as we see in the fulfilled prophecy of the risen Christ, the diverse but unified spiritual body by which God creates and redeems us in His image. And that is the overriding purpose of the church. It is not a social gospel. It is the consuming gospel that will meet beyond our social needs.

God's church is the foundation upon which we script and define our lives... Truth and reality you can build on—God's Church is the real church in an unreal world.

hearing   believing   engaging

I believe in the true church that I see clearly all around us...and the honesty that it demands from us.

If you do not believe in a God of eternal righteousness, then faith would not be of any earthly or heavenly good, would it?

If a world of order and righteousness did not exist, then would anything at all be dependable? Could a cogent science exist... could we have all this technology today without faith to kickstart it into fact? No. Faith is non-negotiable in science. Faith also is non-negotiable in Christ.

REALITY is the world or the state of things as they exist, as opposed to an idealistic or notional idea of them.

Reality. This is my purpose in writing.

Consider with me things in our lives that are non-negotiable... We all come from the same origin of fallen man when we are born.

Do not forget where you came from.

We will report to the same table of reality

What is believable in life?

Here are eight life questions that man has asked down through the ages. We will always need answers to these questions so go ahead and get your life answers ready.

Is there a Moral Law?

Do we have an origin? Do we have a destination?

What do you believe about God the Father, Jesus the Son and God the Holy Spirit?

What is hope?

Can God forgive our sins?

Do you believe in absolute truth?

Where does love come from?

Moreover, here is the question that encompasses all these questions:

Is God just a concept to you? Is God a living reality? Concepts are not enough.

If you believe in a God of righteousness, you are a good candidate for great faith.

After all our questions, there is a reason for faith because faith is reasonable. Faith cannot be separated from anything we do in life.

If you want to live in the real world,

you will need faith in God.

The Holy Bible is that Word of faith given to man in miraculous ways.

It is not man's word, but the Word of God. No other word can claim this from the foundation of the God, who has no beginning or end, and is the God of the Past, the Present and the Future.

Concerning my love for the Word of God, The Holy Bible, it has not always been true. I thank my Pastor, Dr. Melvin McCullough for his vision of challenging me to read the entire Scriptures on a one-year schedule.

Here are six realities from the table of reality the Bible teaches us:

- All Truth belongs to God, the Creator of all that is and will be. We are sinful, conflicted and fallen.
- Our Lord God calls us to submit our divided hearts to Him and be changed.
- God calls us to eternal life and obedience to Him.
- God sees our chronology with His timelessness. Through the death and resurrection of Jesus Christ, His Son, we receive forgiveness of sins to new life by the new covenant of His body and His blood.
- God calls us his sons and daughters. He created us to worship Him.
- Sorrow and evil will cease in God's eternal day.

This is the reason that Christianity is not just another world religion. It is not *like* another religion. It is the miraculous salvation of mankind from the foundation of the world.

Christianity is the real church in an unreal world.

The timeless God of all creation is our Heavenly Father. He is seeking and calling us personally by name. He wants to redeem and remake us in His likeness. He promises us a continuing dialogue.

God does not promise life without grief, sorrow or disappointment, but promises much more: that those who are true will receive the crown of eternal life, which God gives to them who love Him.

This is God's Word to us, His dialogue with us. It is His plan from the beginning. It is our destination.

The prophecy and miraculous birth of Jesus did not start a new religion but was the fulfillment of God's promise to a world He created. We are God's children written into the miracle of life.

My dialogue with the Bible has been a life-changing experience.

I have come to know the reality of a loving God in terms of the past, the present and the future and to know that God is timeless. Only the timeless Creator God can be an intervening God.

Yes, He is a loving and intervening and unchanging God. His dialogue is forever settled in heaven!

Can we actually have a continuing dialogue with God our Father? Yes! Indeed! That is the nature we share. This is reality. How do we

Who is the Lord, the God who demands our allegiance? What are His attributes? What does He say about Himself?

This is our real need for a dialogue with God.

What can we know about the Beginning?

Is it evolution vs. God's Creation?

Some people say the debate of evolution is over, that science is settled. And I ask, you mean like no discovery, no more questions? People who say science is settled stop asking questions. It is not a matter of faith anymore? Seriously? Do you believe this? Scientists disagree with you.

God gives the story, the facts. He says, if you want to live in reality, you need faith in God. Go discover, take dominion of the earth. Believe by faith. Keep asking questions.

I believe the Bible answers all these questions. Moreover, we have evidence. Without God, science cannot give a logical or cogent answer without raising more questions. Where will we find our answers?

If you really want to understand God's answers for your life, ask the Holy Spirit to open your eyes to His Word. Start the dialogue. Ask. Let God answer. The dialogue with God will begin.

As a man thinks, so is he. (Proverbs 23:7)

We cannot be neutral if we expect to escape the insidious nature of our culture. It is true, even more than we realize.

We live in a noisy, complicated social and computer-driven culture. We have information overload; we induce influences and pressures on our lives. It hides and distorts the beauty and truth God wants to show us. Our thought life is easily hijacked. We need conversation with our Maker and Creator.

THE BITTER TASTE OF REALITY
LANDING AT THE WRONG CONCLUSION

Perhaps you remember the Southwest Airlines 737 that made a clear night landing at the wrong airport in Branson, Missouri. That runway is 3,740 feet, and only half of the length of shorter runways needed for normal legal operations.

How can pilots land at the wrong airport?

How can many things happen when intelligent people make assumptions? Can a pilot be certain he is landing at the right airport? Is there absolute evidence available?

The operative word here is *assumption*.

Like the Southwest pilots, I have been in flying situations many times, and assumptions in aviation are dangerous. Again, dialogue is needed to overcome wrong assumptions.

The handoff of Air Traffic Control to visual flight conditions ends with the words "radar services terminated." This puts the burden of orientation and navigation primarily on the flight crew, where it should be.

Approaching Branson, these pilots proceeded with wrong assumptions. *Matthew 24:24 gives a warning: "Even the elect can be fooled."*

It does not take Satan to deceive us. We can deceive ourselves.

A faulty dialogue will always land us at the wrong conclusion.

My answer: It is quite easy to land not knowing where you really are. Of course, there was no excuse. It was a grievous mistake. The pilot's dialogue before landing was faulty and useless. Southwest Airlines is a great airline, but like all pilots, we are not exempt from mistakes. We have all said, "There go I except for the mercy of God." It is true.

hearing   believing   engaging

This thought can be provoked even by a little reprimand on the radio to a pilot to "Listen up!"

I was not there for the Branson landing. However, I can write the likely scenario, having been in that situation many times: a visual night landing, not an instrument approach.

No doubt, the night visibility was good and the pilots saw the runway several minutes ahead. A shorter runway is often narrower and can make the runway look longer from a distance.

Bright runway lights will always change our focus. Bright lights add to the invitation. A runway seems like home to a pilot. Consider this:

The flight crew was well trained and experienced.

They were proud of their impeccable flight experience and record.

They had executed similar landings hundreds of times in varied weather and visibilities at hundreds of airports.

They were not lost (in their minds).

They were convinced they had the right airport in sight.

These pilots were legal until they descended and crossed the line of **reckless operation of an aircraft** as defined in Federal Aviation Regulations. (FAR 91.13)

They made the approach, intended to land and did. At touch down, they realized their grave mistake and suddenly became believers of absolute reality.

To their credit, they immediately jammed on the brakes to keep from going over the ravine at the end of the 3,741-foot runway. We are talking about nanoseconds in braking action from disaster. It is amazing that the tires did not blow.

The first conclusions were, "Great job, boys. You saved it! Nevertheless, sorry, you're fired." I understand they retired. However, they are responsible and the judgment was pilot error.

It is not air traffic controllers that night or the person who might have turned the runway lights up bright.

It is not the team that designed the airplane or wrote the training manual.

Simple pilot error, case closed. I know this as an airline pilot.

Let me tell you some airline secrets. Keep them to yourself.

They were only seven miles from the truth, however far from reality when they touched down. Wrong airport! Electronic navigation became secondary to an inviting bright runway. Completing the landing checklist was suddenly job number one, to set up a stabilized visual landing while the urgent truth of the inactive and unused flight management instruments silently screamed, "No!"

Where was the dialogue when it was needed? Both pilots had lost situational awareness. One of them needed to step up and call for climb power and gear up. However, neither did.

Here is a list of things that could have happened that night before they landed at the wrong airport. Some of these are good things. However, good things can be a distraction.

Similar runway orientations at nearby airports. Airports are built this way because of prevailing winds.

It might have been the pilots' first night landing at what they assumed was the correct airport. It was not a tower- controlled landing. It does not matter. They made other mistakes before they touched down.

They probably announced a flight advisory that the airport was in sight and flew a visual approach to land (at night). (Oh yes, it is legal procedure and done all the time.)

There could have been a lack of radar vectoring because no radar facilities and/or tower operations available at the time of landing. (Again, legal and all common procedure).

Approach control might have said, "Radar vectors discontinued, you are cleared for a visual, (approach) good night." This reinforces the assumed fact that all is well.

However, it really means, "You are on your own, Captain!"

Yes, I have made many visual approaches at night. It only feels good when it is completed and you did it right. Now, consider my speculation of other factors (physiological, psychological and philosophical).

The prevailing visibility (an aviation term) was fairly good at the time. They were seeing everything. Their lack of diligence operating by the familial rather than the expedient. Failure to follow available backup information. visual, written and electronic. The runway visual picture "Looks right to me". Crew fatigue, perhaps. However good pilots do not spectulate.

Forgetting speculation, let us talk truth and reality.

The rocks and hills and various temperatures around Branson or any airport makes visibility variable, night and day.

However, at seven thousand feet and fifteen miles away, it can be a snare to call the runway in sight because it looks right and even more convincing as you get closer and lower. In this case, the pilots were looking at the wrong airport and did not realize it. When it is all over, yes, we always go back to truth and reality. That is when we can admit we were either wrong, lied to or misled. And besides, the runway looks like home to a pilot!

And there it is: physiological, psychological and philosophical factors. Liberated thinking! That is how we get into trouble.

How easily we get diverted and distracted from truth and land at the wrong airport of conclusion and our passengers ask, **"What happened?"** We never intend it. However, as with any life situation, we are not exempt from being responsible.

I prefer truth and reality to any alternative liberation. You can land at your own conclusions, but first consider how easy it is to be deceived by knowledge and preconceptions.

Whatever your vocation, we all live and fly in night darkness. We live in a culture that refuses to believe the truth, tell the truth and tells us to blame other people for our circumstances.

In the Gospel of John, Jesus talked all about this with his disciples. He knew they had to get their theology right. He knew His disciples faced wrong conclusions about their purpose and mission. He was teaching them to "go into all the world", the Great Commission. Allow me to paraphrase.

In Matthew 10:14 (my paraphrase) *Jesus said, Be vigilant. Do not trust yourself or even what you see. Pray for wisdom. I will tell you what to say when you need it. Don't land here! Shake the dust off your landing gear and go to the next town if they do not receive you.*

And somewhere in the Bible, God must have said this: "You can be the sharpest knife in the drawer and still get cut or deceived. Just believe me. I AM God, the God of the first and the last word."

These pilots were looking at the wrong airport, and their flight navigation system could have easily confirmed that fact. They lost situational awareness. It was the bitter taste of reality.

They were having a pleasant night until diligence was lost.

Somewhere before the landing one of them needed to say, "No! Let's get out of here! Let's do a missed approach now. "Let's shake the dust off our wrong thinking."

I wonder what thoughts and questions they have today? They selected the wrong airport. It was a dreadful reality.

hearing   believing   engaging

GOD SPEAKS TRUTH THROUGH HIS WORD

Would the eternal God Who created us in His image, not give us a plan (a study guide) for our lives? No. Certainly not. God made us for reality.

So, God gave us The Ten Commandments. And then He gave us much more. Hope! Love! His only begotten Son, forgiveness of sins, Salvation. Eternal Life! We do not have to land at the wrong airport of conclusion.

God spoke then and He speaks now. He speaks great value to us through His Word.

Walmart create its home brand of "Great Value". In this day of radical secularism, we can find great value in living life beyond what we often try to find, like our relentless search for entertainment.

God still speaks. Maybe we should just keep digging around in the Bible, God's Holy Word.

We might avoid landing at the wrong conclusion.

If you want to live in reality, you need faith in God.

There is that word again, "reality." How do we get to reality?

God created us in His image with a spiritual and physical body. We gain *knowledge* in the physical world with things we can see and touch. However, we gain *wisdom* by things we cannot see or touch, and we find reality.

We learn because God made us for reality.

For example, we understand gravity. We know we cannot jump out of a building without injury or death; and God gives us light so we can understand darkness.

Long before we knew it, God began a dialogue with us. He gives us dreams and visions.

It really does not matter at what age we hear God's voice in us. The dialogue is a gift of reality. It is there that God gives us hope, God gives us knowledge and wisdom while leading us to reality. He says, "Love not the things of this world that will rust and decay"

(Matthew 6:19). And His Word gives us many other hopes and assurances.

Our lives have a mission. Clear the deck! Put aside the distractions and make room to hear God's thoughts. Yes, God is reality and leads us to the table of reality.

Jesus warned the noisy crowd during the Passover festival when they misunderstood his purpose and mission. They were living their lives in theological conflict. Jesus replied, *"Walk while you have the light, lest darkness comes upon you, for he that walks in darkness, knows not where he goes"* (John 12:35).

A person who does not know what they believe is in theological conflict. Reality is not on their table and is not required.

However, God is always seated there.

THE GOD OF THE FIRST AND LAST

"I am the Alpha and Omega, the beginning and the end" (Revelation 21:5).

In life relationships, the first and last words we speak in a dialogue with anyone are the most important words we say. The first and last impression we make on each other are the most lasting impressions.

Give people a good takeoff and a good landing and they will not remember much about the rest of a flight.

Lectures and flying are much the same. Start well and end well and most people are satisfied. Mention food at the end, and people will leave with a happy taste in their mouths. We get the point.

So, the question again: What can we know about our beginning? What can we know about our ending? How do we get on the road to reality?

Eugene Peterson, who paraphrased the Bible in *The Message*, speaks of the ageless belief in the creation story in Genesis. In his Introduction he wrote: *"If we don't have the sense of the primacy of God right, we will never get it right, get life right, get our lives right."* ... *"Not God at the margins, not God as an option, not God on the weekends...God at center and circumference; God first and last; God, God, God"* (The Message).

God is the God of the first and last Word. He says what He means and gives us the ability to discover His truth. There is no uncertainty, no interpretation needed. In God's presence, we have no room to vacillate or quibble. Yet we often try.

We really do need to get it right.

Some people believe that scripture reveals only what the reader sincerely discovers it to say, that the Bible is unclear and the certainty of truth is mythological. They disregard the Bible's historical accuracy. However, God does not mumble, because He is reality.

Is there a better example than the story of salvation, His redemption and forgiveness of sin? His authority over life?

The story of Jesus proclaims a miraculous beginning and ending in his birth, death and resurrection. These prophetic stories are actual events in history. His second coming is prophetic as well. The Godhead presides over all because He is timeless and eternal.

Reality! God again will have the first and last word of his creation.

Let us get the dialogue right! God spoke his world into being and will have the final word to the demise of this world and the world to come.

THE ETERNAL METEOROLOGIST

I write now as a pilot and a meteorologist who has seen the clouds from both sides.

God is the Eternal Meteorologist. God's Holy Spirit hovered over the waters in creation and He forecast this world to pass away. The timeless day of eternity will begin where there shall be no more night.

God is in control of climatic events and the balance of the elements. Man cannot control hurricanes, earthquakes or sunspot storms. God, the Eternal Meteorologist, is in charge of His creation and man cannot precipitate or prevent global warming, period. God first and God last. The universe is far too vast for man to control. Man cannot even control his own body!

One volcano eruption can pollute the global atmosphere with more carbon than anything man can do to keep it clean for a thousand years. Besides, our earth's atmosphere is self-cleaning and durable.

Many people do not know that it takes dust particles, water vapor and lifting wind and without these three, it cannot rain: yet rain covers the earth, constantly purifying the atmosphere.

Why the arrogance of illogical and unbelieving man? He cannot control the weather. Not even with desire, invention or "silver iodine" cloud seeding. Let's get real in this matter of physics.

Man does not push the buttons of the universe. He does not say when to be born or when to die. He does not control the balance of nature. This world is but a travel vehicle. Man is only along for the short ride to another destination.

Surely God must have a great sense of humor when He eavesdrops on the thoughts of man.

Whatever our dialogue is with God, we need to get it right.

What are the other questions about dialogue with God?

hearing   believing   engaging

Who is the Holy God who demands our allegiance? What are His attributes and what does He say about Himself?

God is love.

God is light.

God is omniscient, all knowing.

God is everywhere, omnipresent.

God is eternal.

He is God the Father, the Son and the Holy Spirit, the Triune God.

He is the Creator and the giver of life.

Who can know the mind of God?

Is God always calling us?

What is God's power and sovereignty about if it is not faith, love and dialogue?

Can we dialogue with God? Yes. Let us count the ways:

Through creation,

Through nature,

Through our spiritual conscience and intellect,

Through prayer and dialogue.

However, and best of all, what God says about Himself is through His Word of Life to us.

hearing   believing   engaging

THE YES-OR-NO QUESTION

Pilots always do what Chicago O'Hare tower tells to them to do. If not, they get sent to the back of the line!

Most of the time airline pilots only have perfunctory dialogue with the control tower; however, at rare times communication can curtly turn into yes and no.

However this time it was an unusual dialogue of "yes and no" to O'Hare Tower. Usually, (tongue in cheek,) we say "Yes Sir" and "No Sir".

Let's talk about some weak faith . . . and wisdom.

Chicago O'Hare operations were suspended that afternoon as a large violent weather system passed west to east. We were number one for takeoff waiting for the weather to clear and for the airport wind shear alerts to go silent. I had already refused a takeoff clearance shortly before this deluge of rain. The tower wanted a pilot report (flight conditions) and I silently did not want to be their "guinea pig runner".

The rain temporarily let up and the local visibility lifted a bit. After a few minutes O'Hare tower broke the silence and again cleared us for takeoff.

However, I still saw no "virtue" (desire to go through there) on the radar screen in the east takeoff corridor where we were heading.

Two operational questions: When does "**no**" turn to "**yes**"? After all, we do want to takeoff. That is what pilots do. In addition, when does "**I**" turn to "**we**"?

Let me put my airline hat on and I will tell you an airline secret.

Airline captains learn to say "**we**" when a hard decision has to be made so, "**we**" refused the takeoff again. I was bold enough to say "no". "We want another five minutes for this weather to clear."

The tower said, "Ok, taxi down the runway, exit at tango ten and get in the back of the line. I've got other departures behind you that want to go."

That was not the "dialogue" we wanted to hear!

It was then that the airplane behind us announced, "We are not ready to go either. We will wait for this local weather to clear."

Well, at that moment, I felt vindicated. My flight deck was a "holy place" and no voice on the radio was going to change that!

Then at that moment a second deluge of rain and lightning hit. My faith reached an all-time "cockpit high"!

Now we are talking about the REALITY of why we declined takeoff. It was laying the groundwork for FAITH. At that moment, I realized that faith begins as an action.

I also knew that I did not get that wisdom from a flight manual or a Bible. And it certainly did not come from me. I knew that moment of wisdom had come from God. Wisdom always comes from God.

So, the question when does "no" turn to yes? There, on the flight deck of your life when do you start saying "we", rather than "I"? That was faith and wisdom my passengers could trust on that flight.

Dr. Tom Barnard, my mentor, friend and supreme encourager and advisor to many, always gives me truthful and prayerful advice. He once prayed with me these important words of wisdom and faith.

"*Help Renda to exercise faith that others can trust, and then give God all the praise.* Yes! *That is faith, simple trusting, with open hands to God.*" And Tom again showed me how faith is lived out. And to always pray for wisdom.

So, let us talk about faith. That is how believers live.

hearing   believing   engaging

A WONDERFUL DIALOGUE IS BORN

This O'Hare story above gives birth to wonderful personal dialogue. God spoke and we were born with free will and we have the right to say yes or no; however, how do we really determine our response and trust to the tower? After all, we are in charge.

The question is: In this current day when virtue is not on the culture's radar, how do we get to the truth of "no" to "yes"?

Answer! You can trust the Lord God to get it right. If disciple Simon Peter can get it right, we all can.

Again, the Word of God gives the good and right answer.

"And for this reason, giving all diligence, add to your faith virtue; and to virtue knowledge..." (2 Peter 1:5)

So, faith begins with diligence? Do you mean "diligence" is faith's starting point? Are you kidding? Do you really mean faith is not mystery, mentality or super spirituality?

Yes! Absolutely! Faith is an action, a decision. Faith is a demand. Faith begins with being able to say "no" when there are storms on the culture's radar. Wait! Do not go yet. The "no" decision might be better than the wrong decision.

I never said that faith was easy, but at that moment my faith hit a cockpit high as a bolt of lightning hit a half mile down our takeoff runway!

What causes lightning? – severe friction of up drafts and down drafts- not something you want to happen near the ground.

So, what about my weak faith? We had done the right thing waiting!

If you remember anything about Simon Peter, the tempestuous disciple of Jesus who had denied His Lord three times, but now he is Peter the Apostle of God, then you know this is the transformed

Peter speaking in this scripture, not the lying, denying Peter. We do not need a theologian for this, do we?

He is Peter the Rock, the declaration of Jesus himself, and the newly reformed Apostle in dialogue with his Master, the Peter who has proclaimed, "You are the Christ, the Son of the living God." (Matthew 16:16)

Now Peter is preaching a reformed message that speaks important words of life that He learned under his Master, Jesus.

"Giving all diligence" paves the way for virtue and the revelation of knowledge.

It gets even better. Knowledge leads to Godliness and Holiness.

Here are Peter's easy words of FAITH paraphrased, straight from the scripture, and they are words for our everyday life situations. (2 Peter 1:5) "Now for this very reason also, applying all diligence in your faith.

give moral excellence virtue,

and in your moral excellence, knowledge,

and in your knowledge, self-control,

and in your self-control, perseverance,

and in your perseverance, Godliness."

Please follow me through this wonderful scripture ... it goes all the way back to our delayed takeoff at O'Hare that afternoon.

Do you see what has happened to Peter's faith? It all leads to Godliness and Holiness.

Just to think, a couple of years before, Simon Peter's weak faith had been rebuked by his Master who said to him.

"Get behind me Satan!"

And then the stinging dialogue when Jesus said,

"Before the cock crows three times, you will deny you ever knew me." (Matthew 26:34)

However now by the power of God, the Apostle Peter is preaching this message:

"Add to your faith, goodness and to goodness, knowledge and to knowledge, self-control and to self-control, perseverance and to perseverance, godliness and to godliness, holiness . . .

As I have stated before . . . Captain, your "life deck" is a holy place . . . and the most holy place in your heart where there is no place for peripheral distractions. And so, I say, "If there is lightning in your life right now, do not takeoff. Wait!" Do not leave the safety of your refuge.

What an amazing scripture. If we go forward to 2 Peter 1: verse 4 we discover this huge and transforming event.

"For by these God has granted to us His precious and magnificent promises, so that you may become partakers of the divine nature, having escaped the corruption that is in the world."

Did you get that? - partakers of His divine nature, and escaping corruption? . . . So, the cockpit story of our lives teaches us . . .

how "no" turns to "yes" and the big "I" becomes "we".

. . .flight story to be continued.

hearing believing engaging

GET IT RIGHT

"But God has chosen the foolish things of the world to confound the wise; and God chooses the weak things of the world to confound the things which are mighty" I Corinthians 1:27 (KJV).

Back to the Story of Creation, Meteorology, and the Story of Faith. Back to reality. Public-school children are told,

"Do not believe this fable . . . Let us teach you how man can control he weather." The question is: Who is in charge of the elements of creation? The earth's atmosphere? Global whatever? Warming or cooling? Guess what! They both happen. . . God is in control. And world weather?

Who created the faith that scientists demonstrate in their research? Let's get it right!

The first words of Genesis: "In the beginning God created the heavens and the earth. And the earth was without form and void. And darkness was upon the face of the deep . . . and God said, let there be light and there was light." . . . and somehow . . . it all led to life of plants and animals. And the social scientists say, "No, my children! Do not believe that simplistic story."

But wait! God is the subject of life. God is the foundation for living. God is all about life, and how to really live a God shaped and God filled life. No theologian needed here, either.

God is in control of His Creation. That seems to be easy faith for me because of God's action as the Creator of all things. If not God, then who.

God was first before all things . . . with everything, His Creation. That includes us, all his creation.

God is always present. **Let us get it right.** God was first to split the atom. God is in control of his master plan, the climate, all the interior and exterior forces acting upon the earth and his universe, its elements, its revolution, its evolution, the precession of its axis, its future, everything! God is in control of it all. We need to get it right.

hearing   believing   engaging

If I know anything at all, I know meteorology. I know weather. It has been my constant study over 21,000 hours in the air while flying many thousands of people to world destinations. It is water vapor, dust and wind. I have seen the hand of God everywhere.

"Water vapor and wind"! The disciples observed this phenomenon firsthand in their boat when Jesus commanded the wind and sea to calm down.

"And with fear they said, *"Who is this Lord that even the wind and sea obey him?" (*Mark 4:41)

What is weather if it is not wind, dust and water vapor in the atmosphere? God is in control of weather, not man. **Lord, I fervently pray our children are taught this truth.** Protect them from foolish and unfounded teaching that would make them trust you less and not believe in You, the Creator.

The book of Proverbs is one of the greatest dialogues in God's Word. Read its wisdom for all its worth.

"Trust the Lord with all your heart and lean not on your own understanding. In all your ways, acknowledge Him (give Him control and power) and He will direct your path . . . Draw near to Him. (Proverbs 3:5)" The bottom line is this:

Lord, make us at peace with your creation. We have to get the Genesis story right. God is in control of His Creation. We observe His weather dialogue every day. He did not leave that up to man. Mere man cannot claim that sovereignty. Man did not and cannot create the physical laws of the universe. Though they may try, this evidence cannot be duplicated or fabricated.

hearing believing engaging

THE STORY OF JOB

Consider this well-known story to make the point.

God needed a good man that He could trust to have a running dialogue about his Creation. God knew where Job lived. You know the story.

Satan said, "Let me test him. I can make Job curse you." God said "Go ahead, you can have everything except his life." Then Satan went to work. After Job was severely tested, Job was spent. He wanted to die but he had been true.

Maybe, just maybe, here is the reason Job was tested . . . **we all know the purpose of tests . . . to see if we have the right answer.**

Then the Lord spoke up, (Chapter 38) "Job, listen up. I need to tell you a few things." Maybe God even said, "You along with millions who will follow you, need to get the story right."

Job,

"You were not there when I (God) laid the foundations of the earth and flung the stars into the heavens.

Man does not know how its dimensions were created, and who did the surveying.

Man was not there when I defined the boundaries of the sea and clothed them with clouds and darkness.

Man was not there to command the morning to appear,

Nor does he know where the gates of death are located." (Job 38)

What wonderful words from the Word of God!

God is the source of all of it; the rotation of the universe . . . of all science, physics, mathematical formula and knowledge . . . of all wisdom, of time, the past, present and future. He created the volume of the oceans and the thermal dynamics of the earth and heavens. Can the fact be clearer?

We will not get it right, unless we get God right, and get right with God. Never! Nada! Zilch! . . . Wherever our dialogue goes, we need to get it right.

This is a day that demands great faith and purpose. This is a day for courage . . . courage of a different kind that we are called to exercise, like never before . . .

Like Job in the Old Testament, God has seen these times in the past. He has seen disobedience and idolatry, and He has called his children back.

God has seen the falling away of the splintered church, He has seen his people spent and He has restored them.

God gave us the day of Reformation, churches of common ground amid insignificant differences. He gave us great schools of higher learning, seminaries and Bible colleges. It is all in God's plan for us.

God wants us to get it right. It is imperative that we get it right. God is the God of the first and last word even when the culture says no.

We are never so good, so qualified that we do not have to humbly confront the Gospel of Christ.

(I love these words of Eugene Peterson in his Introduction to Genesis; The Message)

"If we don't have the sense of the primacy of God right, we will never get it right, get life right, get our lives right." . . . "Not God at the margins, not God as an option, not God on the weekends . . . God at center and circumference; God first and last; God, God, God."

ENCROACHING DARKNESS
AND LOSS OF VISIBILITY

Consider this story of a flight from San Diego to Cleveland one afternoon. My First Officer was flying this leg.

We flew at 35,000 feet, just smooth, clear air and visibility unlimited for four hours, never a thought within thirty minutes, of having to land on a dark foggy runway with very little visibility. (it was not in the forecast)

Then, as night fell, descending through 8,000 feet with a beautiful clear vision of Hopkins International Airport in sight twenty-five miles ahead, and cleared for a straight-in visual approach, the cool gentle breeze started blowing in from warm Lake Erie. We saw it develop rapidly . . . The temperature and dew-point suddenly merged together and we scrambled to shoot a low visibility ILS landing into the fog bank the last dramatic 3 miles.

We touched down with minimum forward visibility and rolled into a dramatic 1/8th-mile visibility turn off the active runway with no forward visibility for taxi. What a time not to be lulled to sleep, with legal minimum fuel remaining, and unsuspected evening ground fog clinging to the runway. (What a sudden surprise it was)

Here is my spiritual application. Are we being lulled to sleep by the politically correct ruse of the culture?

We cannot be hijacked or taken in by the politically correct culture that has invaded our thought life and practice.

What kind of Christian pathway would that become? (And the pc culture gleefully says, "We are right on target. Bullseye!)

So, whether a believer or a skeptic of these words, read on and consider this analogy of human behavior and thank God, knowing that God's physical laws mimic his spiritual laws as well.

THE MAGNETIC COMPASS

The magnetic compass is the pilot's basic guiding instrument for navigation. It aligns to magnetic north with known places on our map and measures the magnetic angle that the plane is flying. It requires no power other than from God's magnetism laws buried forever in the elements of the universe and points to the true course. God's power.

The radio and television soap, <u>The Guiding Light</u>, was another magnetic compass measuring "human behavior". This syndicated show went off the air in 2009, after its initial beginning in 1937 on national radio.

Why?

In a world of new permissiveness and the redefining of family values and morals, this yesteryear TV soap lost relevance among today's audience and culture. The wholesome connotation of the very name of this TV series came from a prevailing world view that reflected our Christian moral compass of behavior.

Here is my analogy.

We all have a "moral compass", a spiritual compass buried deep in our human heart. It is God's unchanging natural law and requires no power other than the drawing magnetic forces of the Spirit of God and His Word from the Creation of the Universe.

However, like the human heart, the magnetic compass reacts to flight forces which induce inherent errors.

For example, if an airplane is in a turn or changing airspeed, the magnetic compass temporarily skews off the true heading and indicates a false heading. The plane must be in stable flight for the magnetic compass to indicate correct headings.

In much the same way, our changing culture denies the moral compass of human behavior and skews the true course. What once was deemed right, is deemed wrong and what once was wrong can be reasoned to be right. Yes! Just another way God's physical laws brings truth to Gods' unchangeable spiritual laws.

You can be sure that Satan and evil will try to take you off course to a predicament or place you would not recognize and never want to go. That is why Christ followers need to be aware of the attraction of the culture.

Thankfully, the enlightened pilot and true follower has an additional **slaved magnetic compass** which is correct at all times when it is calibrated and slaved to a stable and known compass heading. The turbulence and unstable forces of flight do not change or affect its indications, and it can be trusted in all flight conditions.

In the same measure, our hearts can be slaved to God's mercy and grace, and when we are rooted and grounded in the power of His Holy Spirit, the turbulence and unstable forces of evil cannot shake us. They cannot separate us from the Love of God.

This is good news! Christians know this as Redemption and Repentance. Through God's forgiveness, we can "slave" our compass (ourselves) in submission to God's Truth so that the turbulence and headwinds of life do not take us off course. As we align our will with His Will, we can then trust God's unseen hand in all of life's conditions. The compass always points to the Father the Giver of Joy and Faith. Faith that overcomes momentary doubt.

"He has also set eternity in the hearts of men; yet they cannot fathom what God has done from beginning to end" (Ecclesiastes 3:11).

"There is a way that seems right to a man, but in the end, it leads to death" (Proverbs 16:25).

John 10:9 says, "I am the Way, the Truth and the Life. No one comes to the Father but by me."

What is your SPIRITUAL compass heading? Is it in alignment with True Heading. Is your heart slaved to the unshakeable forces of God's will for your life?

The magnetic compass is a perfect application of God's natural law and points directly to the spiritual law that God has implanted into man, His highest creation.

THE NATURAL AND
SPIRITUAL LAWS OF GOD

I write now to the power of reasoning to one seeking truth.

... Consider God's natural and spiritual laws and their astounding comparable truth for our lives.

"I will put my laws on their hearts and write them on their minds" (Hebrews 10:6) This is more than meets the eye.

If you are unsure or outright skeptical, consider the *Natural Law* of God, alongside His *Spiritual Law* that He has written into the hearts of mankind. We know this even without His Holy Word. Neither do we have to be a scientist. We understand because we experience these laws every day.

The *Natural* Law of the Universe is broad and extends deep and everywhere into God's Creation. It is never in conflict with God's Creation and always points to the revealed dialogue of Creation and the *Spiritual* Laws that God has written in our hearts and on our minds.

How broad and deep can we go? How logical and how true can God's Natural Law, be? God's physical laws are inexhaustible.

Let me just mention gravity. Every day we live we are under the grip of gravity.

We need not go any further, however we could... Gravity is mathematically true and inerrant and in balance. Gravity is unbreakable and it results in forces that act upon all objects in motion. Yes, force can overcome gravity and inertia. Otherwise, everything would be stationary.

As a pilot in early training, I experienced weightlessness for about fifteen seconds, followed by G forces that I care not to experience again. I strongly believe in God's natural law of gravity. How is that for perfect balance and to be at peace with gravity.

However, there is a backside to weightlessness. We call it "G forces", of which we have no ultimate control, again proving the perfect balance of God's Natural Law.

"G forces" alone will make you believe in the invisible eternal God of Creation, and when you do, you will come to believe there is much more to the spiritual side of the dialogue that God makes available to us through science and research.

These laws are true, in both His excellent Word of Life, and the amazing observance of His inner and outer universe that He allows us to discover.

God's Natural Law is this: Life begets life. Chemical formula produces chemical formulae. Newton's third law is easy to experience: For every action, there is an equal and opposite reaction.

God always shows up, with eternal evidence of the absolute truth of his unbreakable natural law. In the same way, God's spiritual law is true and proven. We need to look no further than the First Commandment:

"I am the Lord, your God (and) You shall have no other God before me."

These two statements go together, the Law that protects, and the Law that commands.

God speaks, and our response is dialogue. God's Word always presents us with dialogue.

This commandment may well be the strongest statement in God's Word to us. Remember, we are discussing both God's physical law...

"I am the Lord, your God", in other words, " You are subject to my natural laws."

And the law written in the hearts of man... I have given you the truth from the beginning, *"Thou shall have no other God before me."*

Because in finality, we cannot. Every knee will bow and call Him Lord.

Atheists have nowhere to hide in God's Natural law because God's Natural Law speaks absolutely of absolute truth, and of Himself.

We are never more moral than when under the spell of God's Natural Laws suspended between Earth and Heaven. Just consider an uncontrolled fall off a small ladder.. . . . and we have not even mentioned *light and heat* and the universe of *energy and matter*. Nor have we talked about the precession of the earth on its wobble rotation (like a spinning top, every 26,000 years or so?) Can man, made in the image of God the Creator, effect climate change, or are there other forces going on?

While we are discussing God's laws, show me a true scientist who does not believe and is not forced to exercise faith in science and discovery?

I quote C.S. Lewis from his book, The Abolition of Man. "**God's natural law** *is not one among a series of possible systems of value. It is the sole source of all value judgements. If it is rejected, all value is rejected. If any value is retained, it is retained. . . The effort to refute the natural law and to raise a new system of value in its place is self-contradictory. What purports to be new systems, all (ideologies) consist of only fragments from the natural law itself."*

"The human mind has no more power of inventing a new value (system) than of imagining a new primary color, or, indeed, of creating a new sun and a new sky for it to move in."

C.S. Lewis *(The Abolition of Man)* 1943; Chap 3 pp.72-80- pp.84-85.

We have just begun to tap the marvelous realities of the natural law of God. Man will never discover all of God's sciences and technologies. What a wonderful thought!

"I will put my law in their minds and write it on their hearts."(Jeremiah 31:33, Hebrews 10:16) These laws are the revealed breathe of God in our hearts.

THE REVEALED DIALOGUE

The revealed dialogue of God's eternal Word is preserved for us. His laws are written on our hearts. We can see and now know what a miracle God performed in protecting the Holy Bible from destruction and decimation. It was like breathing for God. He uses the natural laws to pass along the spiritual laws.

He told us His *Word is everlasting,* and the dark ages of history proved it true ... And the miracle of human life created in His image ... it is also eternal. Because of the resurrection of Jesus, the grave is not our permanent address.

Even if the Holy Bible did not exist in its form of today, we have His laws written on the hearts of all mankind!

The second verse of the Bible says, "And the Spirit of God was hovering over the face of the waters." (Genesis 1:2) Remarkable!

The first words of Genesis and the last words of Revelation are wonderfully related. They speak of the first and last day before the eternal day. There will be a last day before the eternal day. He is God of the first and last word, and the first and last day. God spoke the Natural Law. Notice the first and last words of the Holy Bible. These words are too wonderful to read!

Genesis - "In the beginning God created the heavens and the earth. Now the earth was formless and empty, darkness was over the surface of the deep, and the Spirit of God was hovering over the waters. And God said, "Let there be light," and there was light. God saw that the light was good, and He separated the light from the darkness. God called the light "day," and the darkness he called "night." And there was evening, and there was morning—the first day" Genesis 1:1-5 (NIV).

Revelation - "Then I saw a new heaven and a new earth, for the first heaven and the first earth had passed away, and there was no longer any sea. I saw the Holy City, the New Jerusalem, coming down out of heaven from God, prepared as a bride beautifully dressed for her husband. And I heard a loud voice from the throne saying, "Now the dwelling of God is with men, and he will live with them. They will be his people, and God himself will be with them and be their God.

He will wipe every tear from their eyes. There will be no more death or mourning or crying or pain, for the old order of things has passed away Revelation 21: 1-7 (NIV)."

Then the invitation: *"The Spirit and the bride say, "Come!" And let him who hears, "Come!" Whoever is thirsty, let him come; and whoever wishes, let him take the free gift of the water of life.*

I warn everyone who hears the words of the prophecy of this book: If anyone adds anything to them, God will add to him the plagues described in this book. And if anyone takes words away from this book of prophecy, God will take away from him his share in the tree of life and in the holy city, which are described in this book. He who testifies to these things says, "Yes, I am coming soon." Amen. Come, Lord Jesus.

The grace of the Lord Jesus be with God's people. Amen." Revelation 22:17-21 (NIV).

This is the revealed dialogue of the natural and spiritual laws from the first words of Genesis to the last words of The Revelation.

It is where we enter the stage. We are part of the story. We can enter the dialogue. This is written to believers and those who wish to believe. The dialogue is straight from the Holy Word.

MORALITY AND POLITICAL CORRECTNESS

I sometimes wonder, what is the result of our unwillingness to speak to our convictions, when the fact is, truthful dialogue can strengthen our resolve and clarity.

Intellectual dishonesty is on the rise today in our culture. It will make a man deny the truth and say it is false. It will make him deny he said those words as he hears them played back to him.

Political correctness gives cultural approval for intellectual dishonesty. Just remember, yes and no, they both encompass Truth. Our free choice is the only thing that makes anything a moral issue.

MORALITY AND THE LAWS OF PHYSICS

Honesty and reality go together. If we are not honest, we cannot believe in reality. The laws of physics tell us the truth. So, we need to tell the truth! Yet, we smile and try to take honor for being politically correct and it does not compute with truth. What a riddle!

I can hear in my mind, my big friend, Dave, (who could pick me up and throw me like a football if he wanted to,) laugh and say,

"You big fake! Are you for real? Do you mean, morality and lying go together? Tell me what you know is true in your heart!" And I believe we have to answer.

"There is nothing virtuous in lying or any other dishonest speech."

Morality is God's reality.

Consider this supreme riddle.

Truth and morality is like saying, "when push comes to shove".

hearing   believing   engaging

A tug pushes the airplane off the gate, but our engines shove us down the runway. There is a big difference when push comes to shove. Pilots are different souls when they go airborne.

We are never more moral than when under the spell of God's Natural Laws, suspended between Earth and Heaven.

I once flew with a Captain who had a bad attitude both on the ground and in the air . . . something gone wrong here. It was a quite uncomfortable. Honesty and teamwork is an absolute necessity when flying together. However, that is another story and subsequently, I never flew with that Captain again.

Yes. We are different souls once we go airborne.

TRUTH AND VALUE SYSTEMS

I have found that many pilots, and people in general that rejected their religious upbringing in their youth, like to talk religious memories. Here is one occasion describing this supreme riddle.

As we sat in the cockpit waiting for weather to clear, Bill, my flying partner and good friend, opened one of those conversations from a layover dinner the previous evening. He said he felt a deep desire to talk it out, since we had the time to do so.

He began, Renda, our religious backgrounds are similar but I left home after high school and got away from church.

"What's true for you is not necessarily true for me. People can't put their value system off on someone else." I smiled and replied,

"Bill, you are baiting me." . . .

You see what is happening here . . . **"value system"** has replaced the word **"morality"** and this, like many other words, has changed in favor of an individual neutered expression, which avoids the etymology of the original word, morality.

I continued... "Captain Bill, you just gave a good example; it is politically incorrect to talk about **morality**, but we can call it **personal values**. It is not **abortion**, but it is **free choice**. After all, they say a women's body is **her own**. However, it seems clear to me, that our free choices are the only thing that makes anything a moral issue."

How strangely illogical is our "thinking"... Or should I say is our "dishonesty".

I replied to my Captain friend, "Bill, as I said last evening, my value system is not something I made up. My values come from a Christian morality that God has actually given to all humans through his Natural Law. We are free to choose how we deal with these laws of the heart, but our choices are not without consequences. Murder, cheating, lying, robbing, adultery, dishonesty..."

Then we got into a discussion about how some people think God is the sort who is always snooping around to see if anyone is having a good time and is ready to zap them.

No doubt, you have heard this argument. Perhaps this is a holdover from our childhood or youth conflicts. It seems to be our first reaction in protecting our lifestyle or actions instead of dealing with our "inner voice."

If we can justify the internal false voice that speaks from somewhere inside us... or if we can change the meaning of the word from *morality* to *personal values*, then it does not matter what choices we make as long as they do not hurt anyone else. Then we can place this choice into the category of "political correctness" and that should put it to rest. This solution at least seems convenient. Often and sadly, we buy it. However!

Convenience rarely puts anything to rest.

With that thought aside, Bill and I continued our dialogue.

I said, "It is true that the laws of physics determine how a pilot flies an airplane just as surely as the laws of morality, written on the hearts of man, will determine how well he lives his life. We can ignore the moral voice within us only so long."

My pilot friend laughed and replied, "Yes, it is like trying to be honest and lie in the same breath." I laughed hard and said, "That is funny. I must remember that."

We concluded our dialogue with this thought.

"When we get airborne we will make choices about the operation of this airplane according to the laws of physics, as well as preserving our lives and those of our passengers because we are all moral people, perhaps even more so in the air than on the ground! It is true because honesty is no lie when eternity is peeking around the corner at us.

Then I remembered that even our lives are not our own.

"Do you not know that your body is a temple of the Holy Spirit within you, which you have from God, and that you are not your own?" "For you are bought with a price. Therefore, glorify God in your body" (I Corinthians 6:19-20 (NIV).

It is not new that men forget that we are on loan from God. We **do not** choose when we are born, or when we die. However, what we do with our own "airplane" really does matter, even if we do not collide with another airplane.

What is new is this. Society as a whole has withdrawn from the notion that the Christian Church should give us direction and rules into morality and ethics. It is troubling.

Lighthouses of antiquity are still a modern invention . . . Thank God for the true church!

With the 2010 earthquake tragedy in Haiti, and similar events in South America, it is interesting to note that the news media no longer refer to the extraordinary kindness and deeds of compassion of so many church groups ministering there on the front lines, as acts driven by Christian morality, but it is precisely that . . . as it has always been.

C.S. Lewis gives the definition of truth and morality with this statement: *"Really great moral teachers never do introduce new moralities: it is quacks and cranks who do that. The real job of the true moral teacher is to keep bringing us back, time after time, to the old simple principles which we are all so anxious, sometimes not to see."* (C.S. Lewis, Mere Christianity; Book III, Chapter 3)

May I give an example? The purging and destruction of historical statues and religious displays are false and not new moralities. It is done with a different agenda.

What's more, some contemporary, and misguided theologians will tell you that "Social morality and Christian morality are much the same."

However, Christianity does not work that way. Christianity offers salvation for all men and for all times. In that sense, Christian morality and the laws of physics are much more closely related.

"Morality is God's reality."

Christian morality is born in actual deeds of compassion: meeting needs, whereas, social morality says, "Here! Let me tell you how to think." Social morality fails the test. Beware of quacks everywhere!

The humanistic utopians tell us that the God of the universe is fictional. That He is just another god of the heavens and no more real than a stone image of Buddha or a tribal god of past civilizations. He is a tribal god and his moral laws are tribal morality. They say that anything can be sacred in the eye of the beholder.

However, the principle of the Christian moral life is this: The conviction that no one is able to escape the fact that "we are created in the image of the everlasting God" who gave the Moral Law. And that, is the undeniable reality in which we live.

Christians, remember this. We are not taking our "value system" to Haiti. We are expressing human compassion and Christian love, even the Love of God through Christ, prompted by the terrible and exacting natural law of God, the laws of physics of an earthquake in Haiti. Jesus called it "loving your neighbors as you love yourself." That suggests God's spiritual laws as well.

Is there any doubt that morality and the laws of physics are honestly alike? The moral laws of physics cut across all humanity equally and without bias.

I repeat, "Our free choices are the only thing that makes anything a moral choice." However, you may ask, "What about good and evil that seems to plague some people more than others?" The same question arose in the Garden, and with Abraham, and the Prophets and down through history, and is answered in the dialogue forever on the last day before the eternal day.

So, whether a believer or a skeptic,

In finality, truth is what we have and all we have. And it is enough.

Truth. Everyone knows what truth is. Everyone understands what truth means. And pilots as well as anyone. The question is: What do we do with it? That immediately turns us to "faith". What do you trust? Who do you trust?

"Truly, truly I say to you, whoever hears my word and believes him who sent me has eternal life. He does not come into judgment, but has passed from death to life. Truly, truly, I say to you, an hour is coming, and is now here, when the dead will hear the voice of the Son of God, and those who hear will live." John 5:24-25 (ESV)

PART 2

It is wonderful to have faith in something or someone who makes you a promise, and to see that event come to pass.

I remember when I was a young child I wanted a rope swing in my yard. A good family friend promised me he would build the swing. I put my total faith in him. I could hardly wait. When the swing was finally installed in the tree, I knew I was important to him and that there would be many happy hours of play with my friends. I also learned that fair play and gratitude begins in our adolescent years. Our early training and what we wish for reveals our first belief system.

Up to now, our dialogue has been objective and moral. God's natural and spiritual laws do that and we are accountable for our actions.

Falling ten feet from a swing has consequences, just as damaging a relationship with someone.

What we really believe in our life determines who we become and what we practice will print a copy of who we are.

God's natural and spiritual laws teach us absolute truth by faith.

FAITH

Faith will test our belief system of right and wrong.

What we come to believe matters deeply and becomes a conscious matter of faith. Our *Dialogue with God* demands clarity because God's Word does not mumble. I hope we can get into the heart of our faith in the following pages.

It seems imperative to me, that how our faith is practiced and lived out in a dissected culture that no longer believes in absolutes, that our faith and perceptions are supremely important. Follow me through.

We use faith every day in something we can see and touch. "Truth" becomes the object of faith.

"Perceptions" are often mistaken mind games that we give too much credence. It is far too easy to create a concept of faith on false and unproven perceptions. However, this leads us off point. It is not our purpose here . . . Let me quickly put this to rest with this short statement:

Precepts, Concepts, Perceptions and Implications:

"The precepts of the Lord are right, giving joy to the heart. The commands of the Lord are radiant, giving light to the eyes." (Psalm 19:8-9) NIV. This is the Word of the Lord.

Precepts are from the the Word of God. Trust them fully. Do not necessarily trust your concepts or your perceptions and their implications. Ask God to lead you into His truth. Perceptions come from our concepts, and implications drive us toward action. We need to let God's Word speak His truth in our actions and our faith. Otherwise we can quickly get off base.

An analogy: A pilot's checklist is like the Word of the Lord. It is a precept, the truth, A precept is not to be interpreted but performed in truth. Perception is not the way to think of a checklist. We get into deep trouble in trying to perceive a checklist. *"Faith comes by hearing. and hearing by the Word of God" (Romans 10;17)KJV.*

We tend to think our faith, when God wants us to exercise our faith based the precepts of his Word and Promises.

So let's not get off point. Let our faith trust and believe an unchanging God that will lead us from Exile back into his Promise.

What impedes our Christian faith?

It is a good question because we put faith in many things. We live in a frightening culture that would take our faith away, where most things sacred i under attack and religious freedom is up for grabs. What is next?

hearing   believing   engaging

We are seeing civic regulation and laws restricting Christianity and free speech, the desecration of history and Christian values . A Godless culture can lose all rationality. Perceptions and concepts can make faith seem far away. Does this describe the 21st century?

Our dialogue must become more Biblical and urgent. We will consider analogies of Light, Darkness, Science and Christian Faith. Where are we going? The dialogue continues.

SIGN OF THE TIMES

"Looking for a sign from God? This could be it! What do you believe this church sign means?

Are we missing a signpost from God? If it was wrong yesterday, is it right today? Are we missing God's dialogue?

Will we again consider "Good" and 'Evil"? Will we consider Sin?

In our cultural approach to the tenets of Christianity in the last forty years, there is a strange silence from the church world about good and evil and from many leaders and ministers of the Gospel of Christ, when news commentators mention sin more often than ministers.

I believe our silence is a sin before God. You can almost mark the day in 1973 that the church fell silent. God's Word warns us about this compromise, the Supreme Court decision, abortion.

hearing   believing   engaging

And the flood gate follows. . . homosexuality, same sex marriage, persecution of Christians around the world, the attack on Christmas, religious symbols, public displays, The Ten Commandments, the attack on sermons and free speech, political correctness among other enumerations.

"Looking for a sign from God?" Is God trying to get our attention? This could be it.

Living today in our culture, we live as if, "that was then, but this is now"? Do we put God in that category – a kind of tribal God? Ancient civilizations certainly did. The Israelites, God's chosen people did. In that sense, they turned to idolatry, just as we do today.

The question is: do we make a distinction of a God of then, and a God of now? Has God changed? History gives the answer.

Why does God give us history?

I think we all know – not only to remind us Who He is and our fallen condition, but to give us the right answer for our future.

Remember, just as the Ten Commandments were arriving from Mount Sinai from the hands of God to Moses, the Israelites were setting up their smelting shop. "No graven images?" Was it coincidence? No. And one sin leads to another.

What were the Israelites thinking . . . what had become of the God of miracles they had feared? Had they given in to cultural thought? Had they succumbed to prevailing thinking? Apparently global truth had escaped their thought and the dialogue went with it, as they found themselves languishing in the wilderness. What hindered their faith? What is our parallel today?

The Israelites knew that God was not a tribal god, but the eternal God of the entire human race for all time. We know their history. They understood they were to shun evil and pursue good. They knew that to be God's people, they must drive evil out. (Jeremiah 7:23)

However, they had forgotten the God they served. . . scary words.

God said, "You have to have faith, the faith of your father, Abraham. "You have to be a unique and separated nation. I Am God. I have given you Prophets, yet you want Kings. Are you listening to me? And they ended up in Exile, our parallel today.

I suppose we could deduce that tribal politics had led the Israelites to tribal morality. That is the path it always takes.

And one sin leads to another... and we hardly notice it.

Here is a recent question from national columnist, Michael Gerson. He is asking the modern church amid the current sexual scandals...

"What is a politician's (sexually) wandering hand (today) in comparison to maintaining a law of legal abortion (from 1973)?"

What a sad comparism Gerson makes, however there is a reason. Is it because the church has lost the sense of sin, and is succumbing to tribal morality?

Is the reason because today as never before, we live in a technology driven world that takes command of our attention, and we become dull to the unyielding truth, mercy and the justice of God who created everything that is? Or do we no longer believe in a God of absolute truth?

I do not know who said it first, but it is true. "If you do not stand for something, you will fall for anything." Or turned around, "It is easier to fall for anything than to stand for something."

When we discuss faith, the end result is not to understand faith, however it is to put faith into action being assured by God's natural and spiritual laws that action is the best choice available. God's mercy demands no less from us.

Mercy, Justice and Truth are the attributes of God that we can stand upon and trust. God would not make us his highest creation and leave us holding the bag of ignorance.

Sometimes, we read the Scripture with a nebulous attitude when God is speaking directly and pointedly. Moreover, even worse, sometimes we are not aware of God's appearance, or even His disappearance. Are we enamored elsewhere in our daily living? The scripture says, "Those who have ears, let them hear." (Matthew 11:15) (Revelation 2:29)

An example from the story of Creation:

Adam and Eve disobeyed God in the Garden, and they hid when God made His appearance. Then God said, because of your disobedience . . . *"I will put enmity between you and the woman, between your seed and her seed"* (Genesis 3:15).

This scripture is not from a tribal God, but from an unchanging Almighty God of all ages.

The take-away of this Scripture is that we bear responsibility for our unforgiven sin and disobedience, and our withering faith.

Here is a modern-day example:

I do not wish to ever join the silent ones and ignore abortion—and then hide among a placenta, a plethora of many sins when God makes His appearance. Why? Because, abortion is without doubt the greatest sin against God's Creation and is an unparalleled tragedy of our nation in the twenty-first century. And our pulpits are silent? . . .

Why? because someone said "it is now legal and settled law"? So, what happened to sin?

THE SILENCE IS DEAFENING

"What hinders our faith? And what impedes the truth we say we follow?"

It is a fair question for all believers in the modern church.

We do not enjoy talking about sin but if we are to understand faith, we must acknowledge sin. Our silence drives sin from our conscience in enmity against God. What about disobedience? What is the church's responsibility to preach sin? Maybe we no longer have the stomach for it. Maybe it is time for the church to get a "gut check". Practice the truth.

Nothing has changed about faith and scripture. Faith always shows up on the road as action. God always reveals truth. Who has changed?

"For we wrestle not against flesh and blood . . . but against the rulers of the darkness of this world" (Ephesians 6:12).

And if we do not wrestle, could it be because of sin?

Then, when sensitivity pricks our conscience, we resort to trivial ideas of our upbringing, we call it "legalism", the "do nots" of our youth and hardly address the faith issues facing us today.

The danger is, whatever faith we proclaim is useless and our statement of belief is tucked away in silent documents in the middle paragraphs of whatever it is that we say we believe. Again . . . inactive faith.

Let us not get trivially off track. There are important things, both biblical and prophetic to confess about our faith. It is sin that besets (troubles and defeats) us. Some call it the sin of omission. Most of the time it is the hidden sin of unbelief. Simply silence, the lack of faith in action.

Our silence quietly says, "Let God speak, but it is not for us to hear."

Again, the prime example- abortion.

Do we ignore abortion in fear or silence? Does God's Word remain unproven again in our hearing while sin again is conceived in the moral arena of our heart and how we think? Notice that action is not required. Silence is enough. However, we pay the price.

Think about it. Just because the Supreme Court rules 5-4 in 1973 that abortion is legal, does that absolve sin?

And the church goes silent for forty years buying it?

And sin goes dormant and unpreached...?

And the same year (1973) Carl Menninger writes his book to the church, "Whatever Became of Sin", which created conversation but little heat.

Yes. I will ask the hard questions.

QUESTIONS THAT NEED ANSWERS

Is there a worse spot for sin to dwell than in our heart?

If unforgiven in our personal lives and in our thinking and acceptance, then sin flourishes in the larger social arena (culture) where we live. We try to feel less responsible in this arena, as if we are not playing in the ballgame.

How can we say that it is more complicated now when God is warning us in scripture, Genesis to Revelation? We are dealing with the killing of God's most sacred creation, human life, innocent babies made in His sacred image and for whom He came to redeem.

I do not have to state the Biblical and Christian view of the sacredness of human life...

That God made us in his image and likeness, placing eternity in our hearts...

Then God became a baby, taking on our humanness Himself.

He became man, was despised, crucified, risen and now Christ interceding for us at the right hand of the Father.

Nevertheless, except for a few notable bold clergy, and a few Godly national columnist spokespersons, church members at large are silent and satisfied to know their churches official and silent position on abortion and say nothing from their pulpits;   Ever!

The drift of the evangelical people of my youth, parallels this "tribal morality" and cultural acceptance, and has driven a spike between secular and holy living. Our hearts should grieve.

... Are we not able to see God's mercy?

... Are we not feeling God's judgment?

... Are we not joining the dialogue?

Our silence is one of the great "spiritual disconnects" of our church age. How grieved is the Holy Spirit upon Whom we do not invoke and some no longer preach?

As Daniel Taylor suggests in his book, *"The Myth of Certainty"*, we dismiss easily the loss of Christian faith (action) in post-modern social issues. We simply default to silence until the conviction fades. What an indictment.

If we do not believe God's Truth, are we also denying God's Righteousness? Are not these connected?

How can we follow the commandment of Jesus to go make disciples with this silent sin removed from our conscience and proclamation? Our silence is an internal cancer.

The culture will not believe God's Truth until they see the divine difference in the believer that truth brings. Where is our confession? Where is our restitution? Where is our dialogue?

Jesus did not cry, "O Galilee, Galilee." He prayed:

"O Jerusalem, Jerusalem . . . how oft I would gather you, and you would not..." (Matthew 23:37). The church cannot continue inaction without this dialogue with God.

The glory of God departs from us in our silence and God weeps.

God said, because of your disobedience . . . *"I will put enmity in your heart* (Genesis 3:15) and we are paying the price.

Abortion is premeditated murder against God's law and legitimizes the growing evil that will surely reap a whirlwind of violence and terror to all civilization.

Read the Wisdom of the Word from Holy Scriptures.

Psalm 139:13-16, "For you created my inmost being, you knit me together in my mother's womb. I praise you because I am fearfully and wonderfully made; your works are wonderful, I know that full well. My frame was not hidden from you, when I was made in the secret place, when I was woven together in the depths of the earth. Your eyes saw my unformed body, all the days ordained for me and were written in your book before one of them came to be."

Ecclesiastics 3:11, "God has placed eternity in the hearts of all men."

Jeremiah 1:5, "Before we were formed in the womb, God knows us."

Psalm 139:13-16, "God is active in our creation and formation in the womb."

Exodus 21:22-25 prescribes the penalty of death for same as murder.

We cannot write it off to politics or century. Nineteen seventy-three is our year of enmity. Listen to the dialogue of God.

If we vote for people who are a direct enemy to the God of sacred creation that we claim to kneel before, and to whom we call Lord, then we are fooling ourselves. We cannot have it both ways. Jesus said directly to them, *"The truth is not in you".* (I John 2:4).

When Godly people take a "laissez faire" attitude about the horrors and practices of abortion, they are then living in exile from God's righteousness, and the sin of a culture begins to mean little to us. Is this how "God" allows a nation of wicked people to destroy themselves?   He does not need to intervene or "chastise" such a nation with some spectacular, miraculous judgment.

Just as the Israelites did, have we broken God's Covenant in disobedience to His law of mercy, justice and love, and we live in exile from his promise?

The greatest travesty today is not war, but against the placenta of God, the abortion of sixty million babies in the United States alone. The judgment of a just God will surely come upon us!

You adulterous people, don't you know that friendship with the world means enmity against God?" (James 4:4)

We cannot place any law above God's law.

"The Glory has departed" I Samuel 4:22

When the ark of God is taken in the silence of night, the questions remain . . .

Have we written "Ichabod" across the door of our spiritual life? Has the Holy Spirit departed? Can we practice holiness before the Lord without the Holy Spirit?

Do we even doubt that God is in charge of his Creation?

These are questions that need answers from people who say "Lord, Lord".

The warnings continue in Revelation. Who else but God has his finger upon our longevity and the button of time? That day is looming. We must fall on our knees in confession, conviction and repentance. God's Righteousness is not part-time. His Truth is everlasting. What about the silent church? Are we lost? Will we fail to speak?

"Looking for a sign from God?" This could be it.

God's Mercy and Justice

is Unyielding

God's Mercy and Justice is Unfailing

Lord, God forgive us

FROM DARKNESS TO LIGHT

I once was lost but now I'm found.

What does our faith have to do with God's dialogue to us? Matthew 11:25 says that the truth is hidden from those who have seen but do not believe.

Several years ago, a new-hired regional airline pilot was lost during flight and called air traffic control for assistance. What was the first officer doing? I do not know the details of the incident but I do understand that the pilots were grounded and investigated shortly afterward. Airline pilots cannot get lost!

The air traffic controller gave the lost pilot a true heading to fly to a known visual checkpoint and eventually to the airport of intended landing. They knew the theory of flight and something about navigation. It was not enough. Yes, it was active faith that sought a dialogue with Air Traffic Control (ATC) who then directed the pilots to a known location.

If we do not know we are lost, we are living in present darkness. Until we know we are lost, we will remain lost.

The light of God reveals our lost-ness. We may deny and mock God but we cannot "mock" the light of day.

"The mocker seeks wisdom and finds none, but knowledge (dialogue) comes easily to the discerning." (Proverbs 14:6).

What did these pilots learn that afternoon as night approached? Wisdom and knowledge are not the same thing. Likewise, discernment and intellect are not the same.

The discerning person finds God. However; if the intellectual person spends his time searching for God only in confusion and without commitment, he will never comprehend how lost he is. Honesty before God is needed, not intellect.

Without God's light to guide us, we find ourselves in the lost airspace of self-worship.

Difficult checkpoints in life require much more of us than our intellect.

Sunrise is a good place to start

I have seen many beautiful sunrises. Sunrise happens every day when the darkness gives way to light. God calls us to come to the light of day.

We do not easily discern we are lost. However, when we finally admit it, by faith we are able to deduce answers from our lostness, even having no clue where we are. That is the first sign of hope.

Tomorrow's sunrise is a new day. Go for dialogue. Ask questions. Enter the covenant of a new day with faith.

Only God can make the sunrise. It reminds me that Jesus is the risen Son. He is the Light that lights the world. In Him, we see the light and we find ourselves as we really are.

The sunrise every morning shows us the spectrum of light to which we have been given the reasonable knowledge to discover in the study of physics. However, the sunrise reminds us of the faith that is required to live that day with faith in the eternal God who is in ultimate control of His universe, and not ourselves.

"Seek and you will find. Knock and it will be opened unto you" Matthew 7:7 (NIV). Unreasonable faith is not required. Action is required.

The question is, "What does our faith have to do with our dialogue today?

Our dialogue with God demands both reason and faith. The Holy Bible is a book that requires both faith and action. Dialogue followed by silence is not enough, or we will remain lost.

Only God can make the sunrise

A BEGUILED CULTURE

We live in a culture that thinks nothing of breaking the Ten Commandments. The truth is that we do not break the Ten Commandments; we only break ourselves upon the Commandments when we so lightly disregard them.

The Ten Commandments keeps us from the edge of the cliff, protecting us from temptation and danger. By the same measure, we can miss the truth of God's Word when we disregard them and begin to believe in our own virtue and logic.

To see a "Bridge Out" warning sign just before you fly into the river, is too late to take the detour. It is no good in just following the car ahead.

I speak directly to us, the evangelical church of the 21st century. For more than a generation now, we have presented ourselves with a message to change the culture, but who has changed whom? We must not let the culture beguile the church.

However, it is doing that specifically... in sexuality, in abortion issues, in same sex marriage, in political correctness, in entertainment and morality, in education and history and in cultural values that create barriers to Godliness and Holiness.

hearing   believing   engaging

I wish I could say it better. Perhaps I can. . . the culture will beguile us in our concept of sin and rejecting the Word of the Lord.

Are we drifting? Is it just the times in which we live?

In much of this, the organized church seems unaware that something has gone wrong. The allure of "worldliness" once was a caution light, however now, blending into the culture is a green light avenue to church influence. But is it?

Or worse, has our mission to change the culture morphed into pretention as we congratulate our methodology without questioning what has happened?

Something is wrong in the **teaching**, the **preaching**, the **worship** and the **mission** we evangelicals once knew. Even worse, the loss of the power of the Holy Spirit and the miraculous expectations that we once pleaded.

Has relative truth has captured our imagination, our teaching? Has "philosophy and helps" kind of preaching from the pulpit, whom many say is what people want to hear?

I am not so sure. Much of it seems to be well-worn rabbit trails as we have tried to maintain some kind of relevance to the culture. Or is it redefining the sin and sanctity of our life style?

As the great 20th century prophetic writer, C.S. Lewis astutely said in 1940, *"A recovery of the old sense of sin is essential to Christianity. Christ takes it for granted that men are bad. Until we really feel this assumption of His to be true, though we are part of the world He came to save, we are not part of the audience to whom His words are addressed"* (*The Problem of Pain;1940) para 4, page 37*).

God's commandments are a perfect fit for us like a good pair of shoes. When we depart from God's moral law, we struggle because we are in need of redemption.

The fact is, our nature should be receptive to God's nature because He created us in His image. We are at our best when we ask God to forgive our sin and make us holy. By the Holy Spirit's power only, can we reflect his goodness and obey His Word and His Commandments. It is not our goodness, however, the Holy Spirit whom we need.

It is easy to say that we are all flawed, differently in some manner, but no. What we forget is that we are condemned because of Original Sin from the beginning. A flaw is often a soft sell excuse.

Lewis is right. Until we know just how lost we are and remember the old sense of sin that contaminates our will, we forget how miraculous God's redeeming grace really is.

In large measure, we have refused to answer, even to mention the very word, "sin", because people do not want to hear it.

The old sense of sin will open our heart to our need and to the power of the Holy Spirit.

hearing   believing   engaging

THE BEGUILING LIGHT

I have seen several spaces launches from Cape Canaveral, some in the darkness of night. From 38 miles away, as the space shuttle rises above the horizon, the neighborhood lights up like black and gray daylight from the single source of light from the rocket. However, it is a direct light from the launch engine and it casts long dark shadows behind trees and buildings, because, its' light is not diffused into the whole atmosphere.

It is a directional and undiffused light... attractive at first sight. However, it soon looks like a spooky movie of dark moving shadows, instead of a bright wonderful landscape.

It is a brilliant but beguiling light in the dark sky. It flickers and is soon gone as the light source speeds away into space. Beguiling light will let you down. It will leave you in the dark.

On the other hand, when the sun rises, God is sending a message... God says "Let there be light" and daylight diffuses throughout the entire atmosphere. The sun drives all shadows

hearing   believing   engaging

away, covering all dimensions and darkness is dispelled as the beauty of God's sunrise is revealed.

What is God saying? "I am sending you Light."

Jesus, God's Son is the Light of the World. "He was the true light, even the light which lights every man, coming into the world" (John 1:10) (ERV).

The discerning soul knows that wisdom comes when the True Light of God dawns on us. Wisdom overtakes knowledge; Our faith becomes fact.

God gives wisdom when we seek Him.

There is more than just knowledge to find. Knowledge is not enough. God gives wisdom when we seek Him.

Misapplied knowledge takes us to a wrong conclusion.
The message is *"Seek and you will find. Knock and it will be opened unto you."* We need the discerning Holy Spirit to lead us to the true light of God.

"If we walk in the Light as He is in the light, we have fellowship with one another and the blood of Jesus Christ cleanses us from all sin" (I John 1:7).

"The Gospel is the power of God unto our salvation, the forgiveness of sins" (Romans 1:16 (KJV).

The Spirit Himself testifies with our spirit that we are children of God" (Romans 8:15-16).

God is in every sunrise ... spiritual sunrise happens when Jesus seeks us. He comes for us every morning. God is there, every sunrise.

Jesus said, "I am the light of the world.
Whoever follows me will not walk in darkness but will have the light of life." John 8:12

As long as there are sunrises diffusing the spectrum of light into beautiful colors, we will know that the eternal God of Truth and Morality is in control of His universe. No other source or ideology can replace the unblemished gift of God's forgiveness given to all who seek Him.

When I see lights in the sky, whether an airplane, space shuttle, the sun or a star, I know I am part of something much bigger than the world I can see.

It is impossible to look at the sun and comprehend its revealing light. We can only know the reality it brings. It is the Light of God. However, temporary artificial light beguiles and casts shadows and will leave us in the darkness.

Do not be fooled by the new atheism. (unbelief from unredeemed and unregenerated thinking)

From symbolism, we descend into universalism and mythology. Faith and fact diminishes in Deism, and we no longer really believe that the miraculous Word of God came into His world as a Person. (a baby, the Messiah, the Christ) Again, Christianity is not symbolism. It is incomparable. It is not moralistic, ritualistic, localized or confinable. It is the miraculous story beginning in Genesis and culminating in Revelation.

At the same time, the Gospel of Jesus Christ is simple and true.

"Jesus is the true light that lights the world. He gives light to all men." (John 1:9)

He calls us out of darkness not to walk our walk, but to guide us to walk in the light of God; to be forgiven and forsake sin and follow Him with our words and our deeds. Follow Him obediently in the Creation He designed us to be.

Here is a dialogue from the Bible, although seemingly harsh, nonetheless it is the very words of Christ himself when he told the rich young ruler to go sell all he owned and then come follow him.

Matthew 19:21 The young ruler came to a checkpoint with Jesus, saying that he had kept the law all his youth. However,

he went away sorrowful. He could not see Jesus, the Light of the world.

Remember the beguiling light from a temporary source in a night sky? ...We try to explain that Jesus did not really mean, "sell everything". However, with that, we beguile our faith with a false source of light, by explaining what Jesus really meant to say. And we go away unfulfilled and even sorrowful.

Dietrich Bonhoeffer, in *The Cost of Discipleship*, explains our wrong thinking this way:

"Never mind what Jesus says, I can still hold on to my riches, but in a spirit of inner detachment. However, Jesus realized the trouble was that the rich young ruler was not capable of such an inner detachment from his riches. He went away sorrowful with a distracted faith."

Remember the Northwest Airline pilots in 2009. They lost track of time, got distracted and overflew their destination by not keeping up with their checkpoints. **Checkpoints** are critical! Do not be distracted.

Explaining away their distractions did not change the fact that they did not hear the multiple calls from Air Traffic Control. They knew the laws and rules of flying, but they were seduced by a laptop. They flew east into the encroaching darkness of the night and missed their destination- a foolish thing for any pilot. It required a 180 degree turn of repentance, back to Minneapolis.

The light of the Gospel is not enabled by our intellect or training.

hearing   believing   engaging

FAITH IS A HARD WORD

As we sat in the cockpit waiting on the weather, Captain K asked me to give him a definition for the word "faith". I suddenly felt like "Barney" from Mayberry. I cleared my throat and thought, Lord help me. Picking up on our dinner conversation last night, I said.

We make "faith" a hard word. We try to make faith into some mental exercise, rules and understanding. However, faith is simply believing and acting on what God says and does.

A good way to see faith is through the lens of God's mercy and grace.

Mercy is not receiving the punishment you deserve to get.

Grace is getting what you do not deserve to receive.

When we can believe this, faith makes sense. Faith is an unmerited gift that we receive, a gift that we open and use. Our faith becomes active. We use faith for living and dying.

Holy Scripture explains how we should live and think about life. **"For we are saved through faith, and not of ourselves. It is a gift of God, lest any man should try to . . .**

However, I could see I was losing Captain K.

Then I remembered observing Captain K's actions of faith that morning in flight operations.

I said, "Captain K, this morning I saw you execute a perfect definition of faith while we were in Flight Operations.

You reviewed the flight papers and flight plan.

You signed the flight plan.

Then we boarded the aircraft and here we are waiting with faith to go fly.

That is what pilots do.

"Captain K; reading the flight papers and signing the flight plan, all that makes no sense at all until we get in the plane and go test our faith.

Unless we are willing to put our faith into action, any gift of faith that we have is useless. Also, we will not get paid!

That is what faith is all about, and you have already demonstrated what faith is." The question is in Whom your faith resides? Our lives are not really ours. We are bought with a price, for the gift of life.

Lord, give us faith for living and faith for dying.

THE MOMENT OF TRUTH

An error does not become truth by reason of multiplied propagations, nor does truth become error, because nobody sees it.
— Mahatma Gandhi

Many times, the moment of truth is a "red line".

Slowly, like the Northwest pilots, we easily find ourselves distracted from the truth of where we are going. Meanwhile we are sitting on the sacred flight deck of truth, playing with technology, iPads and invention, lost in the airspace of self-worship and easy faith, not knowing what we believe and not hearing the Voice that has been calling time after time. Answer the "call"?

These well-meaning pilots passed a red line and over-flew their destination; they were not keeping up with their checkpoints. They were enlightened pilots who flew from light to darkness. The truth was hidden from them.

Meanwhile, while night approached, they entertained themselves with new knowledge. All their new invention led them astray. They knew the laws and rules of flying but still got lost in themselves.

Evangelist Christine Caine tells the wonderful story of buying her young daughter her first flashlight.

In wonder and awe as she played with the light in the bright daylight, she suddenly asked her mother, "Mom, could we go find some darkness?"

The purpose of Gods light is to shine in the darkness. We go from darkness to light so that we can return to darkness with the True Light.

IMPORTANT MESSAGES OF FAITH

How do we remain faithful to the Holy Spirit? Only when we acknowledge His leading and invoke his presence in our lives?

With the decrease in church attendance, there is a dramatic rise of "non-affiliates" with their own brand of spirituality, however claiming no Christian discipline of their own. They are finding their spirituality elsewhere in the culture

With the rise of agnostic thinking, evangelical denominations need to examine their creeds and distinctives if they hope to remain a coherent body of believers.

The true church is already correct in its doctrine. **However, we can lose doctrine of sin** by simply "doing church". Cultural methodology often is the reason, allowing the preaching and teaching to depart the biblical center line of the transforming Gospel. In reality, this has happened in many congregations, who have lost the old sense of sin.

THE MESSAGE OF THE CENTER LINE

Airline pilots have a great affinity for the taxiway center line. They know that the center line is better than all the manipulations of radio transmissions. The message of the center line does not have to be explained.

If you are not on the center line, all other things do not fit correctly, the jet bridge, loading equipment and other adjacent airplanes, parked or in motion.

Staying on the center line of the taxi way is necessary for safe clearance of boundaries and obstacles. Otherwise it's a sure way to end up in the mud or worse. Sloppy and imprecise taxiing simply does not have a place in aviation, or our lives for that matter.

The center line is a spiritual exercise. Although the pilot cannot see his nose wheel, he knows when he on the center line and other pilots can see it. There is safety on the center line. By the same reason, it is not strange that others can see our faults easier than we do.

Most importantly, landing on the center line of the runway is the number one indication that shows the pilot's ability to control the aircraft rather than the crosswind currents taking control of the pilot.

Let me bring this analogy to our current cultural crisis. The present spiritual darkness we face is evidenced by disregard of sacred boundaries, and in political correctness and social engineering from our utopian law makers and humanists. It is like a newly constructed taxiway which denies it even needs the benefit of a center line.

This not so new paradigm was spoken about by the Apostle Paul when he wrote, and I paraphrase,

"For we wrestle not against flesh and blood, but against principalities, (things that are handed to us) against powers, (things forced on us) against the rulers of the darkness of this world, against spiritual wickedness in high places" and we go silent. (Ephesians 6:12).

Sometimes we cannot distinguish daylight from the darkness of life's situations, but we can know where God's center line is and where it takes us.

Navigating the center line is not legalism. It is neither a manipulation from anyone's control tower. **The center line is where you will find God's will. The center line is always ours. It belongs to us. We should follow it to the gate.**

Don't let cross currents control your approach. Live your life on the center line and you will avoid lurking trouble and not get mired in mud. God will do the rest. Redeemed lives love the guidance of the center line. Christians find comfort following the center line because they find the leading of the Holy Spirit there on all the highways and byways of life.

A holy life is the real evidence that we have a saving faith in Jesus Christ and the center line is the holy way.

I John 2:6: "Whoever claims to live in Him must walk as Jesus walked."

THE MESSAGE OF CONTAMINATED FUEL

Contaminated fuel, (impurities and moisture) can cause jet fuel to turn into jelly in sub-zero temperatures at high altitudes. Fuel cannot flow to the engines. The result, engines flameout.

During flight, we have a toggle switch at easy reach, that turns on an internal source of fuel heat, keeping the fuel flowing to the engines and preventing flameout.

Likewise, for the Christ follower, this warmth is the knowledge of the forgiveness of sins and the power of the Holy Flame leading in our lives; not finding our own way but in the power of the Holy Spirit as spoken in the Apostles Creed.

It is not popular to say; however, today's culture is disinterested in what they see and hear presently in religion? What is the answer?

The great need of the confessing church is the power of the Holy Spirit in the lives of believers. We cannot embrace the needs of our culture and be like the culture at the same time. We need to appeal to the culture. However, without the Holy Spirit active in our confessing faith, we will face spiritual flameout.

We cannot serve two masters. (Matthew 6:24)

God's Holy Spirit is the Holy Flame that stokes the fire and intentions of our hearts and minds. It is a wonderful thought. The Holy Spirit is the heat that prevents our cold hearts from indifference and flameout. Yes, we need "fuel heat", the fire of the Holy Flame, if we are to influence the culture.

The Holy Spirit must be center-stage in public gatherings and worship, center-court with the youth, and foremost in the social life of embracing the community. We cannot just assume it to be true but to remind us at the start and at the dismissal of our assembling, and our comings and goings, Not methodology, but the *invoking and benediction* of the Holy Spirit in our lives. If not this, then what else matters?

The spiritual battle for the hearts and souls of our youth is being fought in our culture. It is being waged in political terms, where God has authorized us, his followers to fight the battle. This battle is being fought on the school football fields and student assemblies, and in liberal humanistic political education and philosophical thought. And these forces want to silence the church..

We cannot abdicate spiritual battles to the government, the arts, to entertainment and the trends. Or to the humanists, to political correctness, the whimsical offenses of identity politics and Godless lawyers who are out to capitalize on our timid fears.

From 2008 – 2016 our President declared around the world that America is no longer a Christian nation. And that is true when the Holy Spirit is not present in our lives. Without Him our vision is blurred; our worship impaired and our focus is uncertain.

God's people must believe in the transforming power of the Holy Spirit. Our nation is running on contaminated fuel.

Our message must be pure and clear and warm.

Contaminated fuel cannot be trusted nor will it power our lives.

hearing   believing   engaging

TOOLS FOR CHRISTIAN LIVING

The best faith tools for Christian living are not **philosophical**, (something we confirm to our self) but are **practiced because we believe**. Neither are faith tools found in ideas of culture and art; or that which is explained in our heads. FAITH comes by the action of the Word of God in our lives and **often when we most desperately need it.**

The best faith tools are within our simple reach, that illuminates the promises of God. We simply must demystify faith in our thinking. Faith is something we do, and experience, not something we might first understand. Like light, faith illuminates our actions.

Our Christian Faith is like a toggle switch on an airliner, that we can trust within our arm's reach- for example, switches that illuminate an instrument panel, a toggle switch that turn on strobe lights for aircraft takeoff. A third switch when landing, that gives dimension to the runway environment. All these are like tools for illumination of our faith in the Christian life.

Strobe and aircraft illumination lights are not the kind of lights you want to stare at. They can produce **distracting and false light** refractions up close. In foggy conditions or when flying in cloud **layers or reduced visibility, they can interfere with the pilot's vision and flight scan and thinking.**

These **"flashes of light"** glow back from the clouds into the dark flight deck and **distract** vision. When such a condition occurs, the pilots turn off the strobes to stop the distracting **artificial glow**. Strobe and illumination lights can also make it difficult to see the **real lights** of the runway and can even compromise a safe approach to landing in reduced visibilities.

And so, my analogy. We live in a virtual world where it is often difficult to distinguish between the **superficial thing** and the **real thing.** In our worship we need the real light of God. More than ever, it is crucial for us to be able **to discern between the superficial culture and real truth** without distraction. **True lights** are not a **refraction** but rather are themselves a **real source** of light.

As the pilot well knows, he must not let the **superficial light** interfere with his vision of the **real light.** He turns off the **flashing strobes** to let the darkness reveal even faint true light. In the same way, we need to **reject the artificial** and **believe the real** thing.

It is true in our Christian thinking, our worship and our service. Who can we trust? It is not the **artificial light of the culture** or their **rhetoric** that tells us what we want to hear, but those who believe the true light of God and will boldly speak the truth without fear or compromise.

A dialogue with God always reveals truth.

Faith. Is it thought? No. It is action. Let the scripture speak. God's Word is our greatest tool. We do not need a theologian. We need clarity and action of God's Word.

"There is a way that seems right to a man, (thinking) but in the end, it leads to death." Proverbs 14:12

"O Lord, do not your eyes look for truth?" (action) Jeremiah 5:3

"Send forth your light and your truth, let them guide me; let them bring me to your holy mountain, to the place where you dwell." Psalm 43:3 (action)

"But whoever lives by the truth comes into the light, so that it may be seen plainly what He (Christ) has done through God." John 3:21 (action required)

"In Him was life; and the life was the light of men." (John 1:4)
"He was that True light, which lights everyone that cometh into the world" (John 1:9.)

"He chose to give us birth through the word of truth that we might be a kind of first-fruits of all he created" (James 1:18).

A warning. "There is a way that seems right to a man, (thinking) but in the end, it leads to death." Proverbs 14:12

A pleading "O Lord, do not your eyes look for truth?" (action) Jeremiah 5:3

A solution. "Send forth your light and your truth, let them guide me; let them bring me to your holy mountain, to the place where you dwell." Psalm 43:3 (action)

YES, NO, OR MAYBE

Sometimes we have to say "no" to the culture. We think the word "no" is a bad word, especially to our children. It shuts off communication. It has a ring of finality to it. My young daughters always tried to change "no" to "maybe". Maybe gives a thread of hope, a little foothold.

On the other hand, *"yes"*, has an open quality to it. It offers hope, possibility and encouragement. "Yes" is a great word, but only because "no" gives "yes", its meaning. Psalms 119:89 says "God's Word is forever settled in heaven." God's Word is more radical than we believe. Wow, what wonderful dialogue. Read verses 89-96 (NIV)

89 Your word, LORD, is eternal; it stands firm in the heavens.
90 Your faithfulness continues through all generations;
  you established the earth, and it endures.
91 Your laws endure to this day,
  for all things serve you.
92 If your law had not been my delight,
  I would have perished in my affliction.
93 I will never forget your precepts,
  for by them you have preserved my life.
94 Save me, for I am yours;
  I have sought out your precepts.
95 The wicked are waiting to destroy me,
  but I will ponder your statutes.
96 To all perfection I see a limit,
  but your commands are boundless.

When we can say "no" to man's way, then we can say "yes" to God's way. We have a choice, but His way is best. Yes and no is the way for the repenting church . . . repentance, a good word that we must embrace.

However, I sometimes have said "no" to the control tower for takeoff. It stops the process. It stops communication. The tower does not wait a few minutes and then remind you that you are going to be late for your destination if you refuse takeoff.   The next thing you might hear from the tower is: "Your flight clearance time has expired. Contact clearance delivery on 124.55 for a new flight plan."

Lord, you are the Giver of Life. Help us to put our faith into action. Make it Living Faith. We want to trust You more than ourselves

FAITH AND RELEVANCE

Look at this picture. A cockpit instrument panel is a "faith machine", an airliner, a sermon of truth you might say. Each switch and light that we see controls numerous components, valves, sensors and backup systems located throughout the airplane that we cannot see. They are "feed points" to our faith. They all work together in community, with the things we can see with our eyes.

It is not a perfect airplane however, if it is airworthy, then like a church, everything you see is telling the truth. Live and moving instruments define faith and trust. There is that word, that action. faith.

The instrument panel presents a relevant picture of faith. It is real. We do not have to import relevance into the cockpit. We find it right in front of our eyes. The pilot responds in faith with action.

Each instrument adds relevance for faith to fly. We need all of these instruments to see the total picture.

The picture is clear and relevant to what is happening in flight, and at all times reveals our exact electronic location.

The pilot's responsibility is to interpret and trust his instrument panel. Since flight is not static but moving, the picture changes constantly while we exercise our faith to take to the skies.

By faith, we trust the individual instruments in order to interpret the total picture. Each instrument reveals the truth of our faith, to which we yield. Thank God for the instrument panel in our lives, the church that confirms truth and righteousness that we can successfully navigate with surety.

"Now faith is the substance of things hoped for and the presence of things unseen" Hebrews 11:1 (NKJV). In other words, faith is the substance and is relevant to what we believe.

There is a mistaken notion today in religious methodology that we should make the Gospel relevant to people. However, that would be a form of heresy. That is like misinterpreting the flight panel on purpose. Like the flight panel indicates, the Gospel of Christ is already relevant.

Others go even further and say the Bible is unclear and does not reveal the truth about pressing cultural issues in our lives.
They see the Bible as no better than our U.S. Constitution. However, they are flying a "broken airplane". The power of the Gospel is not man-made, but God ordained.

Although there is an increasing secularization of all things in our culture, the Gospel of Christ is God's creation. We are His by faith and made in His image, to love and follow Him. Whatever faith you have been given, remember, **it is a gift from God. Do not treat it lightly!**

hearing   believing   engaging

All pilots agree with the truth that the flight panel reveals. Let me paraphrase Hebrews 11:1 (the faith chapter).

Relevance (THE FLIGHT PANEL) is the by-product... but Faith ACTION is the substance... the SAFETY of things hoped for and revealing the presence of things yet unseen. Like God, the flight panel is constantly revealing the truth. We are by faith in Christ, his creation. (Hebrews 11:1, my paraphrase)

"Therefore, if anyone is in Christ, he is a new creation; the old has gone, the new has come" 2 Corinthians 5:17 (NIV).

Read the faith chapter: Hebrews Chapter 11. It is a great flying lesson. And go fly in unchanging truth and faith in the Gospel of Christ.

WHAT IS FAITH

Pilots often fly in the "soup". That is, they fly by faith, not by sight.
There you have it. That is faith... flying to clear skies.
"Faith" is often a misunderstood word. I like this quote.

"Faith is resting in the sufficiency of the evidence."
Edward John Carnell

The visibility may be restricted but pilots have faith in the part they cannot see. It happens every time on a foggy landing.

We do not see the whole picture. (Our flight instruments give us reason to have faith). This kind of flying is certainly not for the faint of heart or just the well-meaning.

As pilots, we know that we may only see the ground a few seconds after takeoff and just a few seconds before we land. We always feel more qualified after flying on instruments. That is living by faith.

When you drive your car on a foggy night, as sometimes you must, you exercise the same faith. You do not have to see all the stoplights or the turns in the road immediately, but you trust by faith that they will come in sight as you need them.

By faith, Abraham started a long journey that God had commanded. He looked into the mirror and had no idea of the picture God had framed for him. Yet, he was desperately obedient to faith. (consider his obedience to sacrifice his son Isaac.)

Yet, sometimes in our spiritual lives, we want to see the whole picture before we begin. In other words, before we exercise our faith, we say, "Lord, just show me the whole picture and I will obey you."

The great preacher and Scottish theologian James Stewart (1896-1990) said, **"Christianity is not for the well-meaning. It is for the desperate".**

I like this paraphrase from the book of James: *"Do not merely listen to the word and deceive yourselves. Do what it says.* (James 1:22-24; NIV) Anyone who listens to the word but does not do what it says is like a man, who looks at his face in a mirror and, after looking at himself, goes away and immediately forgets what he looks like."

We need to pray, Lord, take our well-meaning ideas away and give us a kind of desperate faith of obedience to you.

REPENTANCE

God's **sovereignty and power comes to all in repentance.** Some post-modern people get uncomfortable, thinking they need to change their mind but all God's children need "repentance". Everyone needs repentance.

However, when we decide that **truth is not absolute, but relative to each in his own way, then repentance becomes impossible. Is this why we do not mention repentance much in the 21st century?**

Repentance is the warning of a needed U-turn on the highway of life. We have to admit that we missed our way. Go no further in the fog. The bridge is out. Execute a 180 degree turn and you can find the right way.

We would rather turn over a new leaf than **confess and turn in repentance** from our sins. We would rather avoid **restitution** to those we've wronged. Perhaps this is just another way of rejecting God's sovereignty and authority in our lives.

Isaiah 30: 15 (NIV) "This is what the Sovereign Lord, the Holy One of Israel says: Repentance and rest is your salvation, in quietness and trust is your strength. . ."

The fact is, many post-modern men do not believe that God is in control. They believe that truth cannot be known, so why submit to a loving God? **They make the wonderful Gospel of Repentance impossible.** Confession, repentance and submission are rarely seen in many church services. We have invented ways of unlinking spiritual formation with submission and conversion.

We do not "cast the net". We would rather drift toward a personal testimony, doing churchy things, rather than witnessing and testifying to the Holy Spirit's convicting power that is found in our repentance. We would rather "hum" our way to heaven than learn to sing the Songs of Salvation.

Several years ago, I was rehearsing music with a youth praise team, and one student, unacquainted with this common theological term asked me what I meant by a "song of repentance".

I answered, "It's a Biblical term and means turning around, changing your mind and resolving to follow God's leading." It's a wonderful thing.

Repentance mends both our broken relationship with God and with man. Repentance commands Christ followers to live in relationship and community with God and each other. Repentance makes us right with God and gives new hope and life.

Jesus said, "It is not the healthy who need a doctor, but the sick. I have not come to call the righteous, but sinners to repentance." **(Luke 5:31-32)**

We need repentance. Repentance is highly Biblical. If we do not yield to the moving of the Holy Spirit in repentance, then He will let us have it our way. Without repentance we deny our past and reject our future.

Public confession and submission has long been the Biblical sign of Christian conversion as God's Kingdom comes on earth in our confessing faith. Jesus, himself provides the example and commands repentance in his Gospel journeys. From that time on, Jesus began to preach, "Repent for the kingdom of heaven has come near" (Matthew 4:17 NIV).
The joy of public repentance and personal renewal will link us with the future work of the Holy Spirit who goes before us.

What is the work of the Holy Spirit? It is correcting our false ideas when life takes a sudden turn. He leads us to Truth, preparing our way, giving us new life. Satan comes to destroy and confuse, but the Holy Spirit comes to breathe new life into us.

This is the undebatable and clear reason Jesus came to this world the first time and will also come again . . . to receive His redeemed believers into eternal life with Him. Jesus said,

"I have come to call not those who think they are righteous, but those who know they are sinners and need to repent" (Luke 5:32).
Repentance does not mean that "the living" die, but that the dead once again live.

hearing   believing   engaging

UNCERTAINTY AND FAITH

> *Uncertainty* lies before us but our *faith* will not be shaken. The *unknown* sounds its alarm but our *trust* cannot be taken. Our God is *good*. Our God is *mighty*. Our God is *healer*. Our God is *protector*. Our *faith* cannot be shaken nor our *trust* be taken. Because our God is *good*, all the time. And all the time, our God is *good*.

This statement of Faith was written by Lily, my fourteen-year old granddaughter, penned just hours before her sister, Emma had successful brain tumor surgery.

Faith statements build our faith; however, nothing builds faith better than obedience.

Dear Lord, *"give us the true faith of children, so that we may enter the Kingdom of God with like faith"* (Matthew 8:3).

"If truth be told", we often come up short on faith. We set up our case, our request for God to prove our situation so that our faith will be documented and affirmed. We misunderstand faith. Instead of bringing faith, we look for faith.

The continuing story in Matthew 8:8, records the Roman centurion bringing his faith to Jesus, when he said, *"Master, I do not deserve to have you come under my roof. If you will just say the word, my servant will be healed."* Jesus said to all present, **"Never have I seen such faith in all of Israel."**

What an important Biblical lesson for us! **We are to bring our faith . . . to come in faith to God so His purposes can be done in us and through us.** Often, we do it backwards. We come in our immaturity to God with nothing ventured, hoping He will build our faith.

My analogy follows. Every time I taxi into position for takeoff, I am saying yes to the tower. I am saying yes to the physical laws of the universe. I am bringing my faith. I am saying yes to the future. I am saying Yes to Faith in action.

It is here that faith is exercised. We bring faith through the door . . . to the task. *"Without faith, it is impossible to please God."* (Hebrews 11:6)

Now is the time to put your faith on the line. Believe the dialogue. The dialogue is written in the sands of time from the beginning of creation. The dialogue is the line that passes through the center of the Church, from Adam and Eve in the Garden, and through Bethlehem, the city of David, through the Cross on Calvary's Hill to the Advent of Jesus Christ and everywhere He was and is and will be.

THE LINE IN THE SANDS OF TIME

Many people say they do not believe in absolute truth . . . but there is a line . . . an empirical event, that happened. That event is Jesus, sent from the Eternal Father in Heaven.

Jesus did not come to start a religion or to present a new idea or philosophy. Jesus came to redeem man from his deepest fault and to live in the image of God Himself. In His miraculous redemption there is no other. The complete story is told in the Gospels.

He did not come to make us better persons. Jesus drew the line. He crossed the boundary. He came to rescue, to redeem us from our sin. Jesus comes to us, to celebrate the gift of eternal life and for the time of our life.

The "line" is an incredible story. The line passes through the center of the Church, the Garden of Eden, and through Bethlehem, Mount Calvary, the Resurrection and Ascension, and will culminate on the second coming of Christ on the triumphant Day of Judgment, when all are gathered. It will be a grand celebration, the story of the mercies of God.

Every time we celebrate Good Friday and Easter, we celebrate the Risen Christ Jesus, and we celebrate his constant question to us:

"Who do you say that I am?"

This is not a rhetorical question. It is the "line in the sand", prophecy fulfilled. These wonderful scriptures tell the story of the Good News of Christ.

Isaiah 60:1 – *"Arise, shine; for thy light is come, and the glory of the Lord is risen upon thee."*

John 3:16 – *"For God so loved the world, that He gave His only begotten Son, that whosoever believeth in Him should not perish but have everlasting life."*

John 14:6 – *"Jesus said, 'I am the Way, the Truth and the Life. No one comes to the Father but by Me.'"*

Revelation 22:16 – *"I, Jesus, have sent my angel to testify to you these things in the churches. I am the root and the offspring of David, the bright and morning star."*

Revelation 5:2 *"Who is worthy to open the scroll and break its seals?" Look, the Lion of Judah, the Lamb that has been slain; He is worthy."*

There is a "line in the sands of time" . . . a scriptural reminder, a triple reminder of the coming of Jesus, the Messiah, the coming

hearing   believing   engaging

of Jesus in our hearts, lives and actions, the promise and anticipation of His second coming.

Prophesy and history comes together in God's Word. We have empirical evidence confirmed by faith by those born again in the image of God.
"Who do you say that I am?"
It is a daily question, a question to all of us. Answer that question today.

THE PIECES OF FAITH

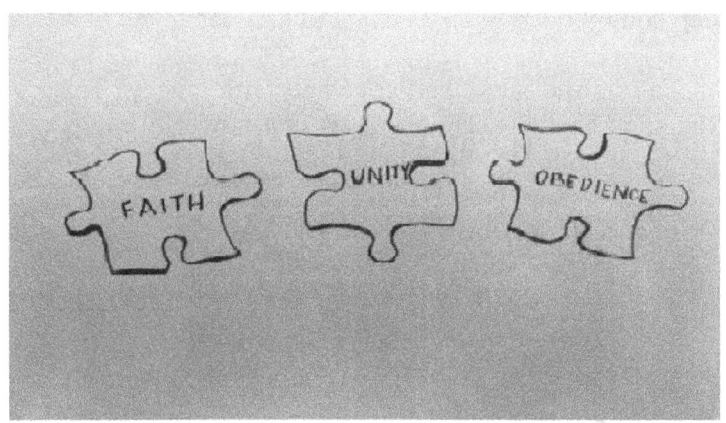

Sometimes, a picture is better than a thousand words.
Let us picture a FAITH puzzle. Keep in mind, this exercise is useless, unless activated by action.

How do you start a puzzle? Normally we say, with a recognizable piece, like a piece of the border of the puzzle.

We are talking about God to where our FAITH is directed. So now, we have the first piece of the puzzle, FAITH.

The second piece of the puzzle is UNITY. That means UNITY in the Triune God, the Father, Son and Holy Spirit.
Deuteronomy 22:10 says, *"Do not plow with an ox and a donkey yoked together."* That is not unity and does not produce the picture of faith.

hearing   believing   engaging

The third piece of the puzzle is OBEDIENCE.

Faith requires the action of obedience

So now we have three pieces of the faith puzzle. Continue to build your puzzle of faith. Without OBEDIENCE, our FAITH is dead. Jesus calls us to follow Him in obedience.

Again, the scripture says, *"In the same way, faith by itself, if it is not accompanied by action, is dead"* (James 2:17 (NIV).

The CALL OF GOD comes first for the Christ follower. Without God calling, obedience and faith have no meaning. Jesus, walking on the water, commanded Peter to come to him. (action)

The call of God puts obedience and faith in sync. That occurs when the Holy Spirit speaks to us. It is a powerful moment. And Peter, the fisherman, left the boat to follow Jesus.

CONTINUING FAITH

I asked a question at the beginning of this book.
"What drives you as you rise each day and put on your shoes? I hope that it is becoming clearer to us.

Faith is a hard word; why even talk about it? Why even go there? Good question . . . It is the same reason pilots still check the weather, knowing they will fly anyway because of continuing faith.

Why go to the moon? Hardly anyone goes there. It is a cold desolate place, isolated, nobody there you know. You need a calling to go there. It is empty and could lose its charm quickly. Does it have anything to do with faith? Yes! Or else, do we try one time, and let the rocket blow up on the pad, and say, well, that is not going to work? No. We exercise "continuing faith".

Faith is not an idea. As I have already said, merely discussing faith is useless. The only reason to have a dialogue about faith is that we will put our faith into action.

I have observed that we try to live our lives self-sufficiently. Sometimes we live as if faith is only an idea, until we are ready, as if there is no action expected from us.

However, the Biblical idea of faith is different than that. If we live by faith, we are pleasing to God. And when we do, it should not surprise us that our joy and happiness level increases. Our praises for God's mercy is on our lips, and our love and obedience to God's purposes and His calling is often on our agenda.

Faith is more than mental ascent. We have to exercise our faith. **We need the community of the church where the faithful, the searching, the broken and the forgiven meet together.**

Faith takes us around the corner, to a new view.
Faith is not just an idea. Faith requires action.
Faith happens on the road. We cannot achieve anything without faith.

Our challenge is to travel light, to be people of faith in an unbelieving culture that is crosswind with most things Christian.

We can easily get faith backwards. Believing when we see.

However, faith is an action word, a decision we make and one we act upon. With the help of the Holy Spirit, **we live our faith in community and relationship,** and in practice, prove our faith. That is forward faith, advancing, active, and in fellowship.

A PERSONAL DIALOGUE

Why do we need to learn the same lesson repeatedly?

Sometimes it takes an unexpected event in our lives to renew our fervent dialogue with God. God sometimes calls us to evaluate our faith.

I experienced such an event recently, when my wife called me on my cell phone and said, "Renda, we need to pray. While you are driving today, pray!" Then she told me why I should pray.

We often say to each other, "We need to pray for this, or pray about that. However, we mostly live around our house as if everything is in our control if we pay due attention to "around the corner events". To be honest, we often live as if we do not need to pray about ourselves. Our tendency is to let our faith lie dormant.

However, that day I felt a desperate sense of dependency. I knew I must pray earnestly. Prayer sometimes is a labor and it is hard because we do not know how to pray when we face the need.

I began to pray, and it seemed a dialogue ensued as if God spoke audibly to me. He said, "Wait. Start with me. Put me at the top of your list." "Tell me again what you have recently been saying about your faith."

"Renda, what do you really believe about my faithfulness to you?"

"God, you made us and know everything about us. I believe you know everything and you can do anything."

"That's good head knowledge, Renda. But if you really believe I can do anything, you've got to move over to the first officer seat now and let me be the Captain."

"Now, what you were saying about my gift of faith to you?"

As I drove, I again cried out my faith to God that I proclaimed. God continued his dialogue with me.

"So, take your faith out of your head and put it on the table. Do you believe I can handle this problem without your help?"

God began to remind me of his faithfulness in the lives of my parents, of my life and my children and their children. He brought this scripture to mind that my faithful pastor, Dr. Keith Wright mentored to me years ago. He had asked me to memorize it with him. I have never forgotten:

"And now just as you trusted Christ to save you, trust Him, too, for each day's problems; live in vital union with Him. Let your roots grow down into Him and draw up nourishment from Him. See that you go on growing in the Lord and become strong and vigorous in the truth you were taught. Let your lives overflow with joy and thanksgiving for all He has done" (Colossians 2:6-7, TLB).

God continued His dialogue with me, *"You have everything you need. You have my Word. You have my promises. What else do you need? That is not all you have. Because of your faith, you can trust me with your future. You can trust me with your family. Everything is in my hands".*

Sometimes we hear the expression, "If you can do nothing else, you can pray," as though prayer were the last resort. However, praying is sometimes the hardest of tasks.

No believer should be surprised that Satan's main object is to get the Christian to restrain from praying altogether and certainly, not to exercise faith.

The words of the hymn are as true as they are familiar --

"And Satan trembles when he sees the weakest saint upon his knees."
-William Cowper 1731-1800

God sees the storm from the other side.

hearing   believing   engaging

He sees the rainbow while we only see the clouds.

KNOWING AND TRUSTING

Here is a story written indelibly on my mind about flying faith.

It was a gusty and stormy night at O'Hare International as we taxied from the gate. Although I dreaded the long night ahead, we had a good view of what was happening as the night approached.

An unfavorable situation was building, that did not promote flying that night because the weather everywhere on the east coast could easily close major airports including Logan World Airport in Boston, our destination.

The evening arrivals and departures were delayed because of a slow-moving line of severe weather. O'Hare Airport remained closed most of the afternoon. Visibility and ceilings were down on the deck, as we say. Hundreds of passengers were stranded in the terminal buildings. It had been a day not to fly to or from Chicago.

Runways 4R and 9R were opening for limited departures; however, incoming flights had been diverted earlier to alternate cities.

Many of the arriving O'Hare passengers had already missed their connections and would spend the night in the terminal. Even

hearing   believing   engaging

if we could fly, most of my 150 passengers would miss their evening connections in Boston.

We were taxiing for departure in a circuitous two-mile line of planes headed for Runway 4 L, which is only 7000 feet long. We needed every foot for a legal takeoff that night. I certainly preferred the 10,000 feet of runway 9 R but that would incur even a greater delay. I knew the particular runway configuration in use would help reduce further delays for many other flights later that night.

In the stop-and-go taxi, I monitored both ground and tower control so I would know how operations were progressing. After two hours of taxiing, we were number two for takeoff. Heavy rain beat down on our windshield. Gusty crosswinds and cloud-to-cloud lightning streaked across the dark, departure-end our takeoff runway. I knew conditions were ripe for the wind shear alert that had been issued.

Often during delays, we jokingly say that we are only getting our nerve up to go fly! That particular night it was no joke. These are the days we like to call in sick... we are afraid to call in scared!

I mulled my concerns about the departure weather and active cold front.

I knew the mixing of warmer air from the Great Lakes and unstable conditions aloft could produce turbulence for most of the flight. However, there are things you can and cannot control in life... an excellent time to put aside the negative contingences and concentrate on the things that we know and trust.

It would be a dark, moonless flight but we had our weather radar. We would go fly.

I knew we had a good airplane because we had flown it into O'Hare earlier that afternoon. We had three perfectly operating engines with no deferred write-ups. Our flight crew was excellent and experienced. We had plenty of fuel and knew our options. Our checklists were complete and now we were number one for takeoff.

I have just described the perfect picture of faith. Now it is time for faith.

After we received instructions to taxi into position and hold, the departing aircraft ahead of us announced a sudden 15-knot loss of airspeed at 800 feet altitude. That was significant wind shear. We had planned a "flaps 25 takeoff" to be legal for the short runway.

Takeoffs were suspended while O'Hare tower monitored the wind shear sensors around the airport. Only when we were satisfied with takeoff conditions would we start down the runway.

There is a time to act and to trust our knowledge when we do not see the total picture. I thought to myself, "This is the picture of trusting faith."

Today we live in uneasy and stormy times, perhaps like never before. We often have a long taxi. We see dark clouds, crosswinds and lightning streak across our path. There is wind shear ahead. However,

These are times to believe the things we know,
And to trust in the One we know. Living as a Christ follower in uncertain days, it is important to know and believe Biblical truth, living our lives in relationship with God's Holy Spirit.

Jesus told his disciples to travel light, that they would be given the words to say when they needed it. He assured them, "... *the Helper, the Holy Spirit, whom the Father will send in my name, he will teach you all things and bring to your remembrance all that I have said to you*" (John 14:26 ESV). Jesus said to his disciples,

"I am the Word of Life.
Trust Me. Believe Me. Follow Me."

What do Christians know?

We live in a post-modern age that makes our faith, truth and honesty increasingly difficult. We sometimes try to make Christianity what we want it to be, like a neo-gnostic idea, but mental Christianity is useless.

If we can recite the Apostles' Creed and not be gripped by these tenants that describe what we believe, then we miss the thrill of faith, much less the future terms and apocalyptic hope it gives.

1. I believe in God the Father, Almighty, Maker of heaven and earth:

2. And in Jesus Christ, his only begotten Son, our Lord:

3. Who was conceived by the Holy Ghost, born of the Virgin Mary:

4. Suffered under Pontius Pilate; was crucified, dead and buried: He descended into hell:

5. The third day he rose again from the dead:

6. He ascended into heaven, and sits at the right hand of God the Father Almighty:

7. From thence he shall come to judge the quick and the dead:

8. I believe in the Holy Ghost:

9. I believe in the holy universal church: the communion of saints:

10. The forgiveness of sins:

11. The resurrection of the body:

12. And the life everlasting. Amen.

I, perhaps like you, have stood and quoted the Creed many times and sat down without another thought about it. However, Please Lord, do not let it happen to me again. Knowing and trusting is gripping faith.

Well, Yes! We did fly to Boston that night ... wide awake with the seat belt light illuminated ... flew an ILS approach, made a nice landing and slept well from four a.m. till noon the next morning. Then we deadheaded back to Chicago and free of flying duty, enjoyed some extra days off. Life is good! God is Good! All the time!

hearing   believing   engaging

WHAT FAITH!

One day I was standing in the gate area having a conversation with a waiting passenger. We were watching our plane arrive at the gate. The passenger said to me, "Captain, I just don't see how that big plane can get off the ground, much less, fly at 35,000 feet. I feel apprehension when I have to fly. I never really feel safe." That was my opening to get philosophical. I replied,

"Well... you know it takes faith to live, faith, to eat your dinner, faith, to drive your car. I told him just to sit and look out the window, look at the wings and engines and feel the power. It is the safest way to go. It is much safer than riding in your car to the airport. Do not worry, we'll get you there."

A short time later, I was sitting in the Captain's seat getting ready to fly to Newark. We were doing our pre-flight checks and from my seat, I thought, "You know, I can only see about ten feet of this aircraft. From my seat, I cannot see the wings, the engines or even see the nose of the aircraft. I just see an area of controls and instruments and a view out the windshield where we are going. If I look back, I only see the cockpit door behind me.

Yet, I have faith that this bucket of bolts and sheet metal that is held together with a million rivets, will stress, bend and hold firm in turbulence and flight conditions. I have faith that it will fly. It is my faith that allows me to sit in this seat and command this aircraft.

It is a common miracle. I am thrilled to be a part of it. Sometimes we get the idea of faith backwards. Wait. Stop! We want to receive first and then have faith. However, faith is more thrilling than that.

Pilots put their faith in their instrument panel.

Where do you put your faith?

It takes faith to believe in the eternal God of miracles. The narrative of faith in Matthew 9: 27-30 reads;

"Two blind men followed along behind him (Jesus) shouting "Son of David, have mercy on us." They went right into the house where he was staying and Jesus asked them. "Do you believe that I can make you see?" "Yes, Lord," they told him, "We do." Then He touched their eyes and said, "Because of your faith, it will happen."

Then, suddenly, they could see. Faith came first, not after the fact. Often, we want to see first and then have faith. Jesus told doubting Thomas, *"Blessed are those who see and believe, but more blessed are those who believe without seeing"*. (John 20:29)

The dialogue of Hebrews 11, the great faith chapter opens with this scripture, *"Now faith is being sure of what we hope for and certain of what we do not see."* What better definition could we want?

Most things in our lives require faith first. It should be easy in our spiritual life as well. Faith is not unnatural. Faith should be as natural as a person walking or breathing. Maybe it is as natural for a man to have faith as it is for a dog to smell the grass.

However, faith is still hard work.

STRETCHING OUR FAITH MUSCLES

Action is required to exercise our faith. It is then that we know our faith is in-sync. Talking about faith encourages us, but honestly, it is practically useless until we stretch our "faith muscles".

Action puts our faith in-sync. Here is a good example, from my own flying.

As Captain, one of my favorite unannounced checklists discovers if my first officer is flying in-sync with me. This requires him/her to be aware of when I intend to start our descent from cruising altitude. When I am ready to call for the descent checklist, I say nothing. I just silently reach for the throttles and pull them to flight idle. If the first officer is observant, he will prevent the landing gear warning horn from blaring. This requires him to stretch forward and push the gear warning silence button on the forward panel as I reduce the power to idle.

Nothing needs to be said. My first officer quickly learns that flying in sync is an automatic task in all checklists items. We call it "staying ahead of the aircraft together". They are better pilots and I, a better communicating Captain.

The New International Version Bible (NIV) says it this way. "Do not plow with an ox and a donkey yoked together." By paraphrase, do not fly with an ox and donkey. They do not communicate together.

Our flight training requires crewmembers to work closely together. It is true that while we may have different personalities, pilots who are yoked together in flight, perform automatic actions together in agreement with flight duties and without distractions. We exercise our faith in each other, as well as the procedures we follow.

If we are Christ followers, we are yoked with Him in obedience and faith, evidenced by our action. I suggest you read Hebrews, Chapter 11, the great faith chapter.

Faith is best understood in action. "Faith is exercised." We bring faith through the door . . . to the task. "Without faith, it is impossible to please God" (Hebrews 11:6).

AN EXERCISE OF THANKSGIVING AND PRAISE

Gratitude is a natural emotion that we express when we want to give praise to someone. We naturally say, "thank you" for gifts and compliments. We really appreciate it." A conversation of gratitude in our daily work and living makes for good will and mutual blessing. It is an easy way to begin a dialogue.

Repeatedly, the Word of God says gratitude and thanksgiving is the starting point of our worship to God. Gratitude is also the beginning of the exercise of our faith in God.

Psalm 100 begins with these words,

"Come into His presence with thanksgiving and His courts with praise. Be thankful unto Him and bless His name. For the Lord is good, and His mercy is everlasting."

Here is an exercise you might try – It is "Counting your Blessings". You may want to do it now as you read this discussion about Thanksgiving and Praise.

hearing   believing   engaging

Here is the exercise:

Consider a normal day in your life. Take a pencil and paper and give yourself 60 seconds to make a list of 15 things you are thankful for... Important hint: the smaller the things, the better and quicker. READ THIS AGAIN TO BE CLEAR.

When you are ready, set the timer and begin your exercise.

How did you do? Was it difficult to get started? I will reveal my first attempt at this exercise. As you will see, there is nothing earthshaking here.

Here is my quickly composed list of things for which I am thankful.

1. Sleep that comes easily

2. Hearing my wife breathe and feeling thankful

3. Coffee

4. Laughter (my wife's sense of humor)

5. Root beer (IBC)

6. "All in the Family!" Mayberry

7. Family, and four grand-daughters

8. The Morning Newspaper

9. Friends

10. Bacon

11. Milkshakes

Then, my minute is up.

Maybe I am beginning to learn that practicing a dialogue of gratitude and praising someone for her ability or kindness to me is an easy habit to form.

Confession is the very act of grace

CONFESSION LOVE OBEDIENCE

Confession is a part of the dialogue with God. God wants our confession. He made us that way. Whether or not we are confessing our faith as fact, or confessing our sins as failure, confessing is good for our soul. Confession transforms our thought life and actions.

Since we are human and have relationships with other people, at some point in our lives we need to say, "I'm sorry, I misunderstood", or "I was wrong". "I did wrong." "Forgive my remark" or "excuse my haste"; "Please forgive me." "You are more important than anything that would stand between us."

Confessing our faults and particularly, our failures in life may be very difficult. However, confessing is always a positive thing because God knows and loves; He forgives and forgets. And by that, and most importantly, He becomes the Master of all good in our lives.

Again, I quote my friend, Dr. Tom Barnard,

"In our human relations, Satan distracts us into confessing our love to each other more often than confessing our faults to each other.

To say "I love you" is much easier than saying, "I was wrong. Forgive me." That's why 1 John 1:9 is as valuable as John 3:16. They go together."

Confession is the very act of grace. It is the purposeful act where obedience and love are born. The Church must always be in confession. Confession is the only way we can keep the first commandment.

This is the dialogue of the three commands from the Lord to Peter in the boat, as Jesus was bringing Peter to confession, love and obedience.

Peter, the disciple, the fisherman, was tending his nets when he saw Jesus His Master walking on the water. He was terrified. Peter loved his Jesus. He said, "Master, if it is you, let me come to you." That was <u>love</u>. As we know, Peter was somewhat impulsive like we sometimes are.

It was the call of Jesus that caused Peter to leave his nets. Peter could have jumped out of the boat immediately, at his own peril, but he waited for Jesus to say **"Come, Peter"**. Then Peter jumped out of the boat. That was <u>obedience</u>.

As he walked toward Jesus, he turned his eyes to himself, "Look, I'm walking on water!", and he started to sink. He shouted, **"Save me, Master!"** That was <u>confession</u> of faith in Jesus to save him. And God took Peter's "heart of stone and gave him a heart of flesh." And by confession, Peter immediately knew.

What is our response to God's grace?

First, it is the call to love God with all our heart, mind and strength. Second, it is our obedience to his call; and finally, the confession of faith and repentance that follows.

I give Peter a lot of credit. His act was not cheap behavior. It was an extreme act of faith. This is how we all will come to the Lord.

Love the Lord your God. Obey his commands, obey his voice, and confess your dependence on Him for life.

Let me paraphrase Dietrich Bonhoeffer, founding member of the European confessing church. In his book, *"The Cost of Discipleship,"* he says, "Unless a man obeys, he cannot believe. Submitting to the church is cheap grace. Submitting to God is costly grace." Cheap grace leads to cheap faith. Costly grace leads to great faith. Cheap grace is dangerous, for it gives birth to unbelief.

Unbelief is dangerous because it gives birth to hardness of heart. Repeated disobedience makes faith quite impossible." See Proverbs 14:10, Hebrews 3:7, Psalm 95:8, Ezekiel 11:19.

Discipleship is not an offer man makes to Christ. It is the call of Christ in love and obedience, giving rise to the confesson of faith and trust. We live generously in the mercy of the free but costly Grace of God. It is a powerful thing.

FAITH DISPELS OUR FEARS

Or is it, fears that dispel our faith? Fear is an obstacle to faith.

What is the mountain that is blocking God's will in your life? Do you fear your inadequacy to believe and to obtain the kind of faith required? Then you are correct on every count. None of us can ever be adequate on our own. It takes more than our efforts. It takes the faith of a child.

God is in every valley and at the foot of every mountain.

James Stewart, the Scottish minister, with his thin tenor voice preached a famous sermon saying "The church is filled with 'no good Christians'". He goes on to say, what the Church needs is Christians with a desperate faith.

The question now becomes, when we will ever have desperate faith enough to say: "Lord, I believe. Please help my unbelief."

Listen to this dialogue from Jesus to the man with the ill son. The man came running to Jesus with his son who had an evil spirit, sudden seizures foaming at the mouth, thrashing on the ground, gnashing of teeth and uncontrolled rigid behavior.) Jesus said, "Bring the boy to me. When the evil spirit saw Jesus, it immediately threw the boy into a convulsion. Jesus asked the boy's father, 'How long has he been like this?' "Since childhood' the father said ... 'Can you do anything, take pity and help us?"

"Can I?", Jesus said? "Everything is possible for one who believes."

Immediately the boy's father exclaimed, "I do believe, "Lord, help me overcome my unbelief!" (John 4:47-54) And the boy was immediately healed. There is a faith that dispels our fears. Lord, help me overcome my fears, my disobedience, and my lack of faith, my lack of action.

THE UNITY OF
FAITH FELLOWSHIP AND WORSHIP

Christian faith does not reside in our mind or intellect alone.

Christian faith resides in fellowship. Fellowship helps to dispel our fears and strengthens our faith. Anything that prevents this unity of fellowship is a stumbling block from Satan himself and true followers of Christ must make a detour around that stumbling block.

The experience of faith, fellowship and worship is the wonderful unity of God and grace, a gift from His hand.

Jesus told the parable of the sheep. There were one hundred sheep in the fold. Ninety-nine were not enough for the fellowship. The good shepherd went to rescue the one lost sheep, and the ninety-nine were blessed and complete. Yes, faith resides in fellowship and our worship is enabled by the Holy Spirit's help.

I recently talked to a man who was afraid to go to church. (He said he was a Christian but did not want to be around hypocrites.) It was pure fear. He does not yet know that Christian faith and fellowship go together, inseparably! I told him he was right. There was no one perfect at my church including me. That is why we attend church. We all have hypocritical tendencies. You do not have to worry about going to my church. You measure up already.

There are timid followers from a distance who have not yet nourished on the wonderful fellowship of believers, those who have not yet begun the dialogue of faith in action.

hearing   believing   engaging

Take the step of faith, pray and believe in God's gift and trust his people, fully. Because in faith and fellowship and worship, we always give thanks. "For the Lord is good. His mercy is everlasting".
What a Fellowship, What a Joy Divine!

The dialogue continues at many other points in the scripture. (John 4:7-8) Jesus speaks of worship. We find faith and fellowship in our worship.

Jesus said to the woman at the well, in this famous dialogue:

"The time is coming when it will not matter where you worship, but how you worship. You must worship in spirit and in truth. Is your worship real? For this is the kind of worship the Father wants from you." (John 4:23) I believe that time has arrived for the church, to worship in truth and in God's Holy Spirit.

We do not go to church to congratulate ourselves . . . or to learn stuff! We go for the dialogue with God and His purposes of our lives. We go to worship, to love, confess our faith and in obedience to the Holy Spirit, and the joy of the Good News.

On the other hand, if we do not exercise our faith with truth, Satan can get us to adjust the terms of our relationship with God. Not only can he get us to yield to temptation, but also make us think we are not being disobedient. Children of God . . . My sons and daughters, the Apostle Paul told us, "For whatever does not proceed from faith is sin."

Faith and fellowship is a part of trusting God's great love for us, and it is synonymous like worship . . . and is worship in the unity of our hearts. Promise God today to worship in Faith and enjoy the fellowship in the imperfect pasture of the sheep.

Worship is the catalyst, the reason and solution to the Christian call to serve. Worshiping and serving cannot be separated. If we truly worship, we will serve. Ministering to the needs of others brings our deepest worship. It is often very painful and calls for carrying burdens that are seemingly without solution. Truly caring in fellowship can revive the evangelical church to obedience.

hearing   believing   engaging

It may require trusting faith and difficult patience when we admit we are not able on our own but are part of the solution and blessings where God uses us in unforeseen ways. It is also an act of worship and dependence, knowing that we must have the Holy Spirit's help to worship and serve as we should.

If you remember nothing else, do not forget Faith, Fellowship and Worship.
I AM the God of solution. Remember I am the God of the First and Last Word.

FINDING REST

"Blessed are you who hunger and thirst after righteousness for you shall be filled." (The Sermon on the Mount)

When you thirst for worship, there is a beauty of God's grace that sustains. Jesus said, "Those who hunger and thirst after righteousness shall be filled."

"Come to me, all you who are burdened and heavy laden and I will give you rest for your souls" (Matthew 11:28) KJV.

"It is not by might, nor by power, but by my Spirit says the Lord Almighty" (Zechariah 4:6) KJV.

God gives us his continuing dialogue. God says, "Pray without ceasing ... call upon my Name. *"Behold, I am with you always, even to the end of the world. Amen."* (Matthew 28:20) KJV

Lord, teach us to pray . . .

. . . Give us your continuing dialogue. Lord, teach us to yield to You. Give us the mind of Faith in action.

Whether going out or in,
Whether lying down or standing,
Whether within four walls, or without,
Give me a thirst for your presence.

hearing   believing   engaging

Give me discernment.

GO OR NO GO

Yes or no? Do we wait or go? Weather exists in both visible and invisible dimensions. Both dimensions can be severe.

Finishing my story about our delayed flight from Chicago O'Hare, let me bring this to rest.

We had refused two takeoff clearances with developing weather in our takeoff corridor. We had been instructed to taxi down the active runway to get back in line and out of the way of other aircraft. O'Hare tower is quick to shut off departures most of the time, when appropriate. This time I was not sure what they were doing.

It was one of those few, but uncertain moments in the flying culture of O'Hare. Our takeoff profile called for an immediate turn to the east. We saw lightning near the runway and departure conditions that we could not ignore. Perhaps the tower did not see it. It does happen. Meanwhile, arriving aircraft continued limited operations on other runways, but then O'Hare is a huge airport. Just because the authorities said we could takeoff, did not mean it was safe, or that we should in our direction of flight.

As I said, it was a holy moment in my cockpit when my interpretation of past flying experience intersected with the future of my flying career. One flight does not make a career. That reality changed our present moment on the flight deck. It took another kind of faith, not to takeoff when cleared by the tower.

Of course, we wanted to takeoff. That is what we do. It is a matter of pride. However, if we had taken off under those perceived conditions based on past experience, we would have been taking off and flying by the seat of our pants on an instrument departure in unknown severe weather while hoping for the best.

I am happy to tell you that is not how airline flying is done. It is always the Captain's call. That is clear. Indeed, this is our reason for additional training in our careers.

Airline flying adheres to a religious mentality and procedures that are not in conflict with any present flight conditions. It is job one to be aware and constantly evaluate severe weather. The pilot needs all things in his remembrance that he has learned. It is the mentality of continuous training. We only takeoff when we are ready!

Consider wind shear or clear air turbulence (CAT). From a distance, you might see the tale-tale signs of wind. However, wind becomes invisible when you are in it and when it takes control of you.

That includes the invisible wind of the times in which we live.

. . . However, to finish the dialogue with the O'Hare Tower that afternoon . . . we were right. It was dark. Severe weather was churning in our climb corridor. After takeoff, we climbed eastbound toward distant Cleveland landmarks and lights that we could not see and radioed back our flight conditions to Chicago Departure Control. We were experiencing severe CAT (clear air turbulence) in cloud layers above and below us.

I said to departure control. "Chicago, don't send anybody else through here. We are experiencing severe clear air turbulence at all altitudes and deviating around the really bad stuff." Yes, it was bad but now we had altitude below us. Based on my experience, it was a good call to wait it out. The weather we could see helped us to transcend the wind shear we could not see.

"Therefore, keep watch, because you do not know the day or the hour" (Matthew 25.13).

Diligence is the operative word.

With that, I realize that I have presented a microcosm of the conflict facing Christians, churches, and religious individuals, belief in a world culture that is in conflict with God's Laws.
However, Culture does not always find coherent answers in our human experience and in the unrestricted freedoms that we seek like when to takeoff, or ignore our conscience or reason in any decision.

Many times, culture and the human experience are in direct conflict. Is this not the reason for a continuing dialogue with our Creator who knows us best?

Discernment enters the spiritual realm. We cannot manufacture discernment. God's Holy Spirit is the Christian source of discernment.

We modern believers often try to live without reliance on the Holy Spirit. We will talk about the love of Jesus and trying to be like him. However even that is impossible without the help of the Holy Spirit.

Here is the critical mass of the Gospel of Jesus- the words of Jesus as recorded in **John 14:26**

*"However, when **He**, the **Spirit** of truth, **has come, He will** guide **you** into all truth; for **He will** not speak on His own authority, but whatever He hears **He will** speak; and **He will tell** you things to come."*

The **Holy Spirit** is the **Spirit of the Living God**. *He does not just* **remind you** *of things you already know.*

I do not propose to discuss reasons other than our culture does not understand the Holy Spirit and, that we live close to that culture and often we live like that culture.

We have fallen away from bringing our petitions for truth and discernment to the Holy Spirit, whom Jesus told us, "When He comes, He will guide us into all truth."

We try to find ourselves and our own way, often without confession or petitions of prayer or invoking the indwelling of the Holy Spirit to give us guidance and power. Impossible.

Our culture will never understand the Holy Spirit. Culture melts when the Holy Spirit takes over.

Church methods must change but Christian worship and daily living depends on the help of the Holy Spirit. This is submission, a term Christ followers know well. He is the Captain. The Holy Bible will never malign the truth of the Holy Spirit. We cannot afford to do that either, by the way we live, worship and serve.

EPILOGUE

When we live without A Dialogue with God, we will live with incoherent thinking all around us that we can have it all, and often unwilling to think we have to give up any of it. However, then the invisible winds hit us and puts us in danger. Perhaps, this is our predicament that God knew in the Garden of Eden when He confronted Adam and Eve.

The societal mentality of entitlement will come full circle. We want careers, family, love, marriage, children, sexual freedom, leisure time, money, credit, debt, (yes debt) entertainment and stuff, never thinking that wind shear is ahead and that God's priority must first be served.

To use an analogy, we need a world view of eternity. We need to stop looking out the side window and look out the front windshield.

If we live ignoring the Past, our Future will fade in search of that eternal Present moment which we try to prolong. Past traditions and experience will hide behind a cloudy and uncertain future if we live only for the now, and our lives will lose the needed lift of flight.

The lesson is this: Man, simply cannot live without A Dialogue with God. We cannot fly by the seat of our own pants.

Do not get carried away by the wind of the times. Meanwhile, live by faith. The action of Faith comes to us when we are on the road, moving ahead, making faith more than thought and putting our faith into action.

THE VISIBLE AND INVISIBLE CHURCH

Every time I board an airplane as a pilot or passenger, I become a part of the "visible airline," but I can see and sense the "invisible airline" on the flight deck. I know the preparations that have been made for the flight. I have studied the Flight Manual.

How do we see the "visible and invisible" church? Let me tell you through scripture.

"The Word became flesh and dwelt among us . . . and we beheld His Glory!" (John 1:14) We can see the majesty and power of God.

John 1:14 is prophesy fulfilled when Jesus became the Word in flesh and lived among us. Romans 1:20 says "For since the creation of the world His invisible attributes are clearly seen, being understood by the things that are made, even His eternal power and Godhead."

He is my Eternal Captain and King.

So: When flying as a passenger, I can feel the parking brake release, I know the airplane papers are now in order and that the airplane is legal and airworthy. I know the checklists verbatim, and I can anticipate the pilot callouts and future flight events before they even happen.

I know the Captain is guarding the takeoff profile in case of trouble. When we hit turbulence, his thoughts are to vacate that turbulent altitude for a smoother flight level. I know he is thinking, "fasten your seat belt" well before it is needed.

I know that my safety is my Captain's first thoughts. I can feel the crosswind on approach, and I am aware of a tailwind on landing. I know because I have been there, with Him.

hearing   believing   engaging

As I sit in the cabin, as a passenger I know that I can endure the visible because my heart is with the invisible.

This is the nature of the Eternal Triumphant Church! It is wonderful to trust the Invisible Church while waiting with the visible church. The deep secrets of God are discovered here.

To speak in a final personal analogy:

Sitting in the Captain's seat waiting at the gate is difficult. We want to start the engines and dispel with the waiting. Raising the landing gear and transitioning to smooth quiet flight is joy and contentment. (That is faith in action.)

I can rest in my faith when I put it into action. Faith is knowing, even without understanding.

My spiritual encouragement comes from knowing fuel is always flowing to the engines that the cabin is continually being pressurized, and the flight path is being protected.

**My faith has found a resting place, not in device or creed,
I trust the Ever-living One, His wounds for me shall plead.**

**I need no other argument, I need no other plea,
It is enough that Jesus died, and that He died for me.**

**My heart is leaning on the Word, the living Word of God,
Salvation by my Savior's name, Salvation through His Blood.**

Words by Eliza E. Hewitt 1891

hearing   believing   engaging

"Now to the King eternal, immortal, invisible,
to God who alone is wise,
be honor and glory forever and ever, Amen"
1 Timothy 1:17

Immortal, invisible, God only wise,
In light inaccessible hid from our eyes,
Most blessed most glorious, the Ancient of Days,
Almighty victorious, thy great Name we praise.

Unresting, unhasting, and silent as light,
Nor wanting, nor wasting, Thou rulest in might;
Thy justice, like mountains, high soaring above
Thy clouds, which are fountains of goodness and love.

To all, life Thou givest, to both great and small;
In all life Thou livest, the true life of all;
We blossom and flourish as leaves on the tree,
And wither and perish—but naught changeth Thee.

Great Father of glory, pure Father of light.
Thine angels adore Thee, all veiling their sight
All laud we would render; O help us to see
'Tis only the splendor of light hideth Thee.

Lyrics by Walter C. Smith – 1867

Someday the seats will be empty in this arena

hearing   believing   engaging

ONE FINAL AIRLINE STORY
Meditation to Empty Seats

We landed in Boston that afternoon with a broken airplane, a pressurization malfunction. Due to the nature of the problem, the return passenger flight back to Chicago was cancelled.

As the passengers deplaned, Flight Operations informed us that the FAA had granted a one leg ferry permit back to Chicago for repairs that night at 10 o'clock P.M. Would we accept the reassignment with pay protection from loss of flying that week? After discussion, my crew accepted the unscheduled night assignment to ferry the plane back to Chicago O'Hare at an altitude restriction of 10,000 feet.

However, the ferry permit also excluded the flight attendants. It would be a noisy unpressurized flight at 10,000 feet, with low level stormy weather along the route and our fuel burn rate would be "out the kazoo". All the seats would have to be empty. We would fly as normally as possible as if we had passengers onboard because that's what we always do.

That night, we decided to keep the cockpit door open for the novelty of this empty late-night flight.

hearing   believing   engaging

Our pre-flight procedures were strange and cumbersome, no people or coffee onboard and seemingly no purpose.

After takeoff, I leveled at 10,000 feet and set cruise power for 350 knots while we flew in and out of night clouds. Within minutes, I looked back and was astonished how empty and noisy the unpressurized cabin was. I decided to walk back into the empty cabin and make some coffee while the first officer flew the plane. It was a weird sort of feeling.

When I returned to the flight deck, I decided that we would close the cockpit door to make it quieter. All those empty seats were an unwelcome sight. After all, passenger airlines operate in community with people relationships... just as churches do, I mean, real flesh and blood on board. When I closed the cockpit door the flight was a little quieter and more normal.

Later when we hit some turbulence, I played the game and turned on the fasten seat belt sign and announced on the cabin intercom "Ladies and Gentlemen, please check your seatbelts and remain seated." We all laughed out loud. I could almost believe I had done a good thing... something like a religious meditation to no one but me!

I remembered this flight a couple of months later when I flew with a pilot who told me he was a religious person and practiced meditation out in nature. He said it made him a better person. He quickly explained that churches were full of hypocrites so he did not attend church. He also did not explain to me to whom his meditations were aimed. And ah ha! I thought of this empty flight that I have described.

In a friendly sort of way, I replied that his meditation seemed to me to be like personally announcing to an empty airplane to fasten your seat belt and remain seated until the rough air passes. I wanted to ask him, "Who is there for accountability?" Easy accountability is popular today. However, I found it strange to fly with no accountability to real flesh and blood in my passenger cabin.

I explained to him that my spiritual life as an imperfect Christian is by necessity, practiced in community with other imperfect people, confessing together to God the Father, the Son and the Holy Spirit, who loves, forgives and empowers us for new life . . . God meets our real need of accountability both in our weaknesses and strength.

This same God offers us eternal life and a place to go when our broken airplane lands.

But sir, you are right. We all need community and dialogue. A broken airplane needs to find a maintenance facility. There is plenty of room in my church for broken airplanes. Even me. And the dialogue is good.

A DAY WITH GOD

God is timeless. That means God goes ahead of us into our future, and back into our past to give blessings, to heal and protect us. God also, is a very present help in the time of our need today. The passing of time does not hinder or tie the hands of God.

Some twenty years ago, my sister, Marlene and I sat down at her digital and acoustic pianos to have fun playing music together. She started reviewing gospel songs that our family had sung as teenagers. With a great memory for detail, she would say, "Remember this one" and we would begin another walk down memory lane of our youth. I hit the record button on the ensemble recorder and captured this special evening.

Little did I know that this event, some twenty years ago would be the gestation of a new CD, *Songs of Testimony and Praise*. She and David, her husband had kept these songs alive in their memory when they would sing them as duets from time to time. These were the tuneful solos, trios and quartet gospel songs of testimony that gives witness to the Biblical imagery that grounds our faith.

What an evening of faith and music review. What a gift she gave to me! I finished the recording process to a full digital CD. Little did I know that God has planted a blessing that would come to fruition twenty-two years later. The blessings of God are not limited in time.

hearing   believing   engaging

I have taken the raw digital tracks we made that evening and with the flugelhorn and cornet skills of my friend Lyle Parker, these songs and words come alive from the witness and testimony of faith-full songwriting saints from the past.

Why should it surprise us how God brings blessings and answers to us after twenty-two years and blessings that last a lifetime.

"A thousand years is only a day to God." Let Him bring blessing and healing to all your days.

hearing   believing   engaging

"DIALOGUE WITH GOD"
Discussion Group Supplement Guide

The primary reason for this discussion group guide is to promote dialogue, faith and fellowship. The truth of God's Word is not controversial but promotes common ground and our vocations raise common questions.

The discussions and questions in this guide are only a starting point if needed. Free free to discuss your own points of interest. Your group coordinator will move the discussions along. Suggested time is one hour per session. A portable microphone is suggested. Munchies promote participation. You may wish to make brief notes in your discussions to help in concise response and takeaways. Keep your individual responses concise.

SESSION ONE _ Read page 15 and 16, PURPOSE 1. Group discussion: Give your best definition of "dialogue"'. 1. List several reasons you would enjoy a dialogue with someone. 2. What moves a good dialogue along? 3. If you were to google the word "dialogue", would it satisfy your practical everyday use of the word? What words or concepts would you want to use to describe dialogue or conversation?

4. What do you do best in a dialogue? 5. Is God's Word more a monologue or a dialogue for you? 6. How we can dialogue with God, name ways it could happen?

SESSION TWO __1. A Dialogue of Reality (page 27-33) is a major theme of Part 1 of this book. 1. Define and discuss reality. 2. What is one human virture that "reality" demands of us? 3. Read "Captain's Prerogative" from pages 21-26. What does a personal prerogative mean in your life? 4. Besides basic needs of life, what are your first thoughts that drive you when you wake up every morning?

SESSION THREE_ **Begin your group session reading the "Yes or No Question" story on page 44.** 1. Share some "Yes and No" situations or decisions you have experienced or faced in your life. Limit your discussion short of question 2 to follow.

2. What reasons or factors played in your eventual decisions of yes, no and maybe. 3. Take a moment to talk about the conflict of this Captain in his difficult weather decision to refuse takeoff clearance a second time from the tower, knowing that O'Hare Airport was operating on other runways. 4. What are the dynamics that enable your decisions of yes and no? How do you feel after you make the decision? 5. What place does restlessness confidence, faith or fear play in a major decision in your life?

SESSION FOUR _A major theme of this book addresses truth and faith. The author draws a strong parallel in both the physical and spiritual laws of the universe concerning relative and absolute truth, p. 56-66.

1. Is it more or less difficult to be objective in a dialogue, if you do not believe in absolute truth? 2. Is morality or objectivity more important to someone who believes in absolute truth?
3. Is scientific theorem or discovery easier to achieve if there are no absolutes to depend upon as opposed to absolutes you believe?
4. Is Good and Evil best defined by absolute truth or relative truth? 5. Concerning understanding and discernment in difficult human relationships, is relative truth more helpful or harmful?

hearing   believing   engaging

SESSION FIVE _ Discuss Christian Living in today's Culture. What are the challenges? **Read the short story of the lost pilots on p. 78-82**

1. Have you ever been lost and did not know you were lost? What implications might this have for today's culture.
2. **Review "Tools for Christian Living", p .93-94** Discuss your thoughts.
3. **Review pages 119-120** (Confession Love Obedience) This familiar story of Peter. How do these actions work in the Christian's Life

SESSION SIX_ Review pages 67-68 and discuss Precepts, Concepts, Perceptions and Implications. What do these words say to your faith?

_Allow the larger group to select several airline stories from the book and discuss together spiritual analogies and God's Word as it speaks to their life experiences. Examples include: pages 21, 34, 44, 53, 110, 114, 116, 125, 132 . In these consider the semblance of God's Word in all our different vocations.

hearing   believing   engaging

SESSION SEVEN__ Contaminated fuel is an analogy of how flameout can occur in the Christian's life. The pilot can see a silent indication before he hears and feels this malady. Read and discuss this topic on p. 101.

1. In what ways can the influence of our culture hinder our living the Christian life?

2. Why do many people not know what they really believe?

3. Discuss your thoughts about the visible and invisible church.

SESSION EIGHT __ Faith is the major Theme of Part 2 of <u>Dialogue with God</u>.

1. Survey the last 50 pages and discuss how you can activate your personal faith and become more vibrant and the ways your dialogue with Gods' Word can grow.

2. Read the Epilogue on Page 128. Consider your world view.

3. With pencils and peanuts in hand, perform the EXERCISE OF THANKSGIVING AND PRAISE p. 118 with your group, Closed book. **Conclusions and Closing remarks**

"Dialogue with God" and *Life at 35,000 Feet* are available on Amazon.com. Church discussion groups can obtain books from the author at group prices. Contact the author at renda@rendawrites.com or <u>rendaual@aol.com</u>

hearing   believing   engaging

Visit RendaWrites.com

A FAITH BUILDING DIALOGUE FROM THE BIBLE

Here is a famous dialogue where faith was born, just three days after the Resurrection of Jesus.

(Luke 24: 13-35) "There were two men, Cleopas and a disciple in deep sorrow when a stranger (who was Jesus) joined them on the seven-mile roadway to Emmaus. Not recognizing him they asked,

"Are you the only person in Galilee who has not heard the news, the crucifixion of Jesus, the prophesied Son of God whom we hoped would be the one who would redeem Israel? It has been three days. The word is out that his body is missing."

That evening with heavy hearts they invited the stranger to stay the night and join them for supper. Then the stranger began a dialogue of the ancient scriptures, beginning with Moses and the Prophets and concerning himself. The stranger took bread and broke it, and suddenly, their eyes were opened and Jesus disappeared from their sight."

Suddenly everything changed. The human mystery was unraveling. A new day had come. The dialogue that Jesus had with his disciples before his trial and crucifixion as recorded in John, chapters 13 -20 was beginning to make contemporary sense.

And from that day and hour, the Good News started spreading into all the world, as Jesus had commanded His disciples.

Jesus asks the eternal question. And, it remains:

Who do you say that I am?

hearing   believing   engaging

QUOTABLES IN THE TEXT

God's word is the password that opens our dialogue box, if we will just "boot up".

It is what it is.

There are no "what ifs" with God

The Call of God is not enabled by our intellect

In all Life, we learn many things by faith And then by fact

Truth is discovered when thought conforms to reality

If you want to live in the real world, you will need faith in God

Yes, God is an intervening God

As a man thinks, so is he (Proverbs 23:7)

A faulty dialogue will always land us at the wrong conclusion

hearing   believing   engaging

If you want to live in reality,
you need faith in God

We really do need to get it right

Lord, make us at peace with your creation

What wonderful words from the Word of God!
God is calling his people to obedience?

Refuse dialogue and feel conflicted

I sometimes wonder, what is the
result of our unwillingness
to speak to our convictions,
when the fact is,
truthful dialogue can strengthen
our resolve and clarity

Morality is God's reality

We are different souls once we go airborne

Convenience rarely puts anything to rest

Our free choices are the only thing
that make anything a moral choice

Lighthouses of antiquity
are still a modern invention . . .
Thank God for the true church

hearing   believing   engaging

Beware of quacks everywhere!

*In finality, truth is what
we have and ALL we have.
And it is enough.*

*Is there a worse spot for sin
to dwell than in our heart?*

*Are we not able to see God's mercy
Are we not feeling God's judgement?*

*Gods' Mercy and Justice is Unyielding
God's Mercy and Justice is Unfailing*

*Difficult checkpoints in life require
much more of us than our intellect*

*Sunrise reminds us that God is looking for us
Only God can make the sunrise*

God gives wisdom when we seek Him

*We need the discerning Holy Spirit
to lead us to the true Light of God*

*A wonderful dialogue
is available to those who seek*

Christianity is incomparable.

It is not symbolism It is not moralistic, ritualistic,
localized or confinable.
It is a miraculous story.

We can be enlightened and still fly in darkness

The old sense of sin will open our heart
to our need and to God's truth

Lord, Start with me!

There is a Dialogue . . .
Written
in the sands of the ages,
It is an event, a prophecy.

Who do you say that I AM

Faith requires the action of obedience

Faith is not an idea

God sees the storm from the other side.
He sees the rainbow while we only see the clouds

Observe nature. You may hear God speak

Faith describes the Perfect Picture

These are times to believe the things we know,
And to trust in the One we know

hearing   believing   engaging

All Faith immediately turns
us toward God Our Creator

Action puts our faith in-sync

Faith is best understood in action

Confession is the very act of grace

God is in every valley and
at the foot of every mountain

Whether going out or in,
whether lying down or standing,
Whether within four walls, or without
Thank the Lord God for His Mercy

Diligence is the operative word

God sees the storm from the other side.
He sees the rainbow while we only see the clouds

hearing   believing   engaging

hearing   believing   engaging

hearing   believing   engaging

www.ingramcontent.com/pod-product-compliance
Lightning Source LLC
Chambersburg PA
CBHW071727090426
42738CB00009B/1898